MEMOIRS OF A JOYOUS EXILE

AND A WORLDLY CHRISTIAN

Memoirs of a Joyous Exile and a Worldly Christian

JAMES M. HOUSTON

CASCADE *Books* • Eugene, Oregon

MEMOIRS OF A JOYOUS EXILE AND A WORLDLY CHRISTIAN

Cascade Books
An Imprint of Wipf and Stock Publishers
199 W. 8th Ave., Suite 3
Eugene, OR 97401

www.wipfandstock.com

PAPERBACK ISBN: 978-1-5326-8004-5
HARDCOVER ISBN: 978-1-5326-8007-6
EBOOK ISBN: 978-1-5326-8010-6

Cataloguing-in-Publication data:

Names: Houston, James M., 1922-, author.

Title: Memoirs of a joyous exile and a worldly Christian / James M. Houston.

Description: Eugene, OR: Cascade Books, 2019

Identifiers: ISBN 978-1-5326-8004-5 (paperback) | ISBN 978-1-5326-8007-6 (hardcover) | ISBN 978-1-5326-8010-6 (ebook)

Subjects: LCSH: Houston, James M., 1922-. | Christian Education—Travels—Biography.

Classification: BX9225 .H60 2019 (print) | BX9225 (ebook)

Manufactured in the U.S.A.   DECEMBER 5, 2019

Dedicated to my children and their families: Christopher and Jean Houston, Lydele and Gordon Taylor, Claire and David Taylor, Penelope and Wayman Crosby

Re: Dis-covered by My Constant Lover

Dear Love! Your love, that flows through Calvary,
Springs through my heart—like fountains in the night—
Flushes clean the dawn, lifelines my drowning plight,
Breaks loose my weighting chains and buoys me free.

Great Mystery! I can but ask, "Why me,
A savage soul, whose life of fumbling flight
Crept underground in catacombed delights,
Remaining shamefully where none could see?"

O Grace! I breathe, inhaling you in me,
Exhaling sighs of thanks for your invite.
You, touching me, dis-covering me of fright,
Transforming lonely "I" to glorious "We."

Entombing deadness darkness rolls away
Reviving Life in Love's embracing way.

John Innes, Vancouver, Summer 1971[1]

1. Unpublished; used by permission of the author.

CONTENTS

PREFACE

*T*hese memoirs are a celebration of friendships, without which there would be little to say.

I am grateful to Bill Reimer, our much-beloved Regent bookstore manager, who not only encouraged me by asking a series of questions as topics for the memoirs, but provided the names of David Paul and Kathy Gillin, to launch the project. Bill is always sending me data on books he thinks might promote my studies; he is selfless and loyal. I thank, for the initial recording of my verbal communication, David Paul, recorder at the Regent College office, without whom the flow never would have started. Then I am grateful to my children, who corrected and stimulated further memories of their childhood. But most of all, I am deeply indebted to Kathy Gillin, who, as editor, shaped the memoirs into a chronological sequence, with a new flow of language that might induce the publisher to accept these memoirs as a substantial historical document. Without Kathy's enthusiasm I might have faltered and given up the enterprise, while her expertise has shaped its accuracy and literacy.

I am also grateful to the staff at Cascade Books for believing in the value of the book, as a small contribution to urge readers to encourage others also, as Paul exhorted the Thessalonian Christians.

As I write this preface, I just came across a letter from my old friend and colleague Bruce Waltke, dated August 20, 1985.

"Are you conscious of chapter LXXXII in the Golden Sayings of Epictetus? 'Ask not the usual questions, were they born of the same parents, reared together, and under the same tutor; but ask this only, in what place [is] their real interest—whether in outward things or in the Will. If in outward things, call them not friends, any more than faithful, constant, brave or free: call them not even human beings, if you have any sense . . . But should you hear that these men hold to the Good [to lie] only in the Will, only in rightly dealing with the things of sense, take no more trouble to inquire whether they are father and son or brothers, or comrades of long standing; but, sure of this one thing, pronounce as boldly that they are friends as that they are faithful and just: for where else can Friendship be found than where Modesty is, where there is an interchange of things fair and honest, and of such only?'"

Bruce Waltke was the very friend who revived the spiritual life of Ernst van Eeghen, who in turn did so much to save the world in his generation.

We all, as readers male and female (which Epictetus's culture did not appreciate), are called to be "the Friends of Jesus," and to be instrumental in his salvific ministry to the world today.

INTRODUCTION

*M*emoir, French for "memory," implies what contemporary writer Karen Luscombe describes as "A looser form of self-reflection, a more experiential and so impressionistic sketch of one's past … their impact is all the more felt due to their capacity to speak to emotion, mystery, and faith."[1] She wrote this in the context of the memoirs of survivors of post-traumatic stress disorder (PTSD).[2] But we all live stressful lives to some degree, so this genre is therapeutic for us all.

For the Christian, memoirs are far more profound expressions of self-reflection, because in writing them, we also stand before God. That is one reason why my favorite poet is George Herbert, whose life has always inspired me. In one of his poems, he meditates upon Colossians 3:3, a verse very significant to me, "Your life is hid with Christ in God":

> *My* words and thoughts do both express this notion.
> That   *Life* hath with the sun a double motion.
> The first   *Is* straight, and our diurnal [daily] friend,
> The other   *Hid,* and both obliquely bend.
> One life is wrapt   *In* flesh, and tends to the earth.
> The other winds towards *Him,* whose happy birth
> Taught me to live here so,   *That* still one eye

---

1. Karen Luscombe, "Out of Trauma, an Impossible Blue," in *The Globe and Mail*, September 6, 2008, updated March 26, 2017.

2. Richard Wagamese, *Ragged Country* (Toronto: Doubleday, 2016).

Quitting aim and shoot at that which *Is* on high:
To   gain   at harvest an   eternal   *Treasure*.[3]

In this profound summary of the paradoxes of the Christian life, George Herbert embedded his memoirs.

Should I, who am no poet, do the same? I have always resisted with some scorn the idea of writing an autobiography. How can one avoid becoming an egotist or a narcissist in doing so? Nor did I ever think my memoirs were worth writing. Let another generation be curious, but I was not. Still, last year I retraced the lives of my parents as missionaries in Spain, bringing along two of my daughters, and that triggered old memories and a new attitude toward the past. I realized I had collected much material in our basements in several homes, rather like keeping tax receipts! I had quite forgotten about their contents. In my book *Joyous Exiles*,[4] I had already written "veiled memoirs," so why not fill them out with a more historical narrative? My training, after all, was in the history of ideas. I was also a tutor, and so mentoring has been my way of life, listening to many live stories. In these rich experiences, I continually found the truth of the adage, "what is intimately 'me' is most universally 'you.'"

Like me, many have suffered from the paralysis of low self-esteem, and so a first motive for writing these memoirs is to encourage others on life's journey. I have also been strongly motivated to communicate transparently, because while I had been very close to one of my two sisters in childhood, I "lost" her when she was recruited for the Enigma program during World War II: she served as a decoding clerk in Hut 6 at Bletchley Park, northwest of London. Sworn to secrecy for thirty years concerning her work breaking German military codes, perhaps

---

3. George Herbert, *The Country Parson, The Temple*, ed. John N. Wall, preface by A. M. Allchin, *The Classics of Western Spirituality* (New York: Paulist, 1981), 203.

4. James M. Houston, *Joyous Exiles: Life in Christ on the Dangerous Edge of Things* (Downer's Grove, IL: InterVarsity, 2006).

one reason she never married was that she could not share with anyone what it had meant to be involved in that work. I have also learned that *fear is the basic emotion* that affects all our human behavior. Transparency is a strong antidote to that fear, opening the heart to receive and to give love.

Secondly, I have lived all my professional life as a tutor, engaging in mentoring students, and they have revealed many intimacies, emotional as well as intellectual. The wisdom I have gained in pursuing the "personal" in the anonymities of our culture has encouraged me to believe that I too have much to share.

Thirdly, I write as a Christian, blessed with a rich heritage of the faith of my parents and friends. I am deeply concerned about the breakdown of institutional religion in churches and colleges. I want to share my experiences, especially regarding the enlargement of horizons—ecumenically, educationally, and emotionally. In *The Narnia Tales: The Last Battle*, C. S. Lewis depicts rising secularism as "the sense of the absence of Aslan." One character has a mystical experience, given to all who truly seek. "Then he breathed upon me and took away the trembling of my limbs and caused me to stand upon my feet. And after that, he said ... I should go further up and further in."[5]

I have interpreted that injunction by the prayer of Augustine of Hippo: "Let me know Thee O God (*further up*), and let me know myself (*further in*)." Perhaps these memoirs will help you do the same.

Fourthly, I have been blessed with long life, nearing my centennial year. Born in 1922, when the thunder of the guns of the First World War still echoed, I have witnessed many changes, now accelerating more rapidly than ever. I have learned it is not enough to be "a joyous exile," as we Christians often feel we are in a secular society, but also "a worldly Christian,"

---

5. C. S. Lewis, *The Chronicles of Narnia: The Last Battle* (San Francisco: Harper/Collins, 1984), 204.

in the sense in which Dietrich Bonhoeffer coined the term—
having responsibilities and stewardship in this world, as well
as preparing for the life to come. This double identity enables
us to be constantly learning new things, as our horizons are
increasingly enlarged.

Finally, I have experienced that you never get "old" if you are
always learning new things, through new friendships and from
much reading of books, old and new. These memoirs are intended
to encourage you, the reader, to keep growing "in Christ" in
the maturity of God-given grace. To cite Lewis again, in *Prince
Caspian*, Aslan explains to the startled Lucy:

> "Aslan," said Lucy, "you're bigger."
> "That because you are older, little one," he answered.
> "Not because you are?"
> "I am not. But every year you grow, you will find me
> bigger."[6]

The more time Lucy spent in Narnia, the more Aslan
seemed to grow—every time he encountered her. She thought he
was getting bigger, but as the I AM, he is always awesome. As he
tells her (and us), rather, it is she who is growing up.

These memoirs are about "growing up."

Christian maturity means seeing the kingdom of God ever
enlarging, while "the self" is evermore diminishing. Even our
churches and colleges need to be envisaged within the broad
horizons of global Christianity, and of the cosmic kingdom of
God. This is as the apostle exhorted the Thessalonian Christians:
"Therefore encourage one another and build each other up, just
as in fact you are doing."[7]

One way in which we encourage one another is by
remembering.

---

6. C. S. Lewis, *Prince Caspian: The Return to Narnia* (London: Collins, 1994), 141.

7. 1 Thess 5:11 (NIV).

Chapter One

CHILDHOOD MEMORIES REAWAKENED, MAY 2017

*T*wo of my daughters, Lydele and Penny, accompanied me on a sojourn through Spain last May (2017), to revisit the haunts of my parents' missionary life.

We flew into Valencia, where I had done my doctoral thesis from 1945 to 1947. Then, by way of an ancient Visigothic castle at Alcaron, we drove to Albacete, the capital of La Mancha, where my parents had lived as missionaries. They arrived in Spain single and separately, and though both were already missionaries, they did not know each other for some twenty years. Mother was forty, Father forty-five, when they married in Madrid. A year later, on their honeymoon in Edinburgh, I was born. They returned to Albacete, where my two sisters, Ethel and Louie, were born. Sadly, both sisters have died: Louie some ten years ago, and Ethel at the end of last year, which awakened many memories of the past, for she was very important in my life.

On this recent trip, I sat on (probably) the same stone seat in the public park under the plane trees where my mother used to sit with the prams for her three small children. We were born late in her life, since she married at forty. All three of us were born after she turned forty-one—miraculously, as you might say, for that generation. Sitting under those plane trees in the center of Albacete, a sudden sadness came over my spirit that I never had experienced before. As in a dream or a mystical vision, I remembered myself as a small boy lying on the tile floor of our simple house, under the couch with its high legs. My little dog and I cuddled together, feeling the sadness of being alone. I suppose that sadness was partially because my father was always travelling around La Mancha for evangelism, while my mother was preoccupied with having three of us in four short years. I suppose this basic childhood wound of "feeling alone" became a compensatory behavior shaping my personality ever since. It has meant that I have always sought out friends.

Some years ago, I wrote an essay for our *Crux* magazine at Regent College: "Exploring the Continent of Loneliness." It has moved many people, as indeed it moved me. The idea of Antarctic penguins crossing an icy vastness has gripped my imagination since childhood, for it is how I felt within myself.

But a second memory was reawakened last May, in another park in Albacete. On exhibition, as a monument of the past, there is a giant railway engine that once was fired by fir logs and hauled the grain, oil, and wine of La Mancha to the Andalusian seaports. As I stood on the step of the railway engine, it reminded me of the faith of my father, who like George Muller didn't belong to a Bible society; he just "lived by faith." This meant he often spent all night in prayer. On one occasion, he had been up all night praying that a member of the congregation, a railway engineer, might remember to pay back a debt so that my father could put food on the table the next day. Sure enough, the railway engineer came the next morning, apologizing for his forgetfulness. That memory and conviction has also shaped my life, that "God answers prayer." My friends and I founded Regent College on the same conviction, forty years later.

At the same time, children of missionary parents commonly find that "the faith of their fathers" can block their own devotional growth; it was so with me. I could never imitate my father's prayer life, and I knew it. I took a "sabbatical" from prayer for many years, finding that even reading many books about the prayer lives of the saints did not help. The loneliness and prayerlessness of childhood were redeemed together when finally I was enabled to experience that prayer is simply a "transforming friendship!" Prayer is like your own fingerprints. It's your own unique relationship with God. Likewise, personal memoirs are not written to be imitated, but to encourage the reader not to be afraid of being one's unique self before God.

That railway engine in Albacete's public park also reminded me of a story our father told us about his missionary travels. He had been invited to perform the marriage of a young Christian couple in a remote pueblo near the Portuguese frontier. As it was a hot summer day in a slow-moving train, Father fell fast asleep, passed his station, and missed the ceremony. Awakened by customs guards, with no return train until the next day, Father went down to the village well, where the women were collecting water to prepare their evening meals. As he handed out tracts to them, one excitedly said, "*Señor*, please come to our home, for my father has been praying for your arrival for more than thirty years." Father was received by an old, blind man, who told him a *colporteur* (book peddler) had given him a Bible, but he had never been able to understand it. Father answered many questions, knowing it was a divine occasion only God could have planned. No wonder George Borrow's *The Bible in Spain* was a family classic in our home; as the agent of the British and Foreign Bible Society in the 1830s, Borrow had sown the seeds for the first evangelical movement in Spain.

Many years later, in Barcelona in 1968, I was the British Evangelical Alliance delegate at the Spanish Centenary Congress celebrating the founding of its first evangelical chapel in 1868. It was thrilling to testify publicly to the heritage of faith I had found in Spain.

Retracing Mother's Single Missionary Life

When Mother was eighteen and living in London, she developed pneumonia. As was medically fashionable in those days, she was told to spend the winter in a warm climate. She was sent to Vigo, in Galicia, in the autumn of 1904. Unbeknownst to her, her future husband was working his passage on the same voyage, not for Vigo, but for Buenos Aires. For as a poor farmer's son, raised in Fife, he wanted to save enough to go to university. He spent five years as a *gaucho* (cowboy) in the Pampas, until a serious bout of malaria forced his return home. He promised God he would be a missionary in "dry Spain," but not the damp malarial Pampas! On his return to Edinburgh, he discovered his younger brother was in financial trouble, so he lent him his savings, though that meant forfeiting his university studies. His younger brother made a fortune in Buenos Aires but cut himself off from the family in Scotland, and he never returned the money.

Father proved himself an accomplished linguist, self-taught in Hebrew and Greek, and fluent in Spanish. He began his missionary life in Madrid, but we have not been able to trace those early years, as he belonged to no Bible society—unlike my mother, who was supported by "Echoes of Service" in Bristol.

Mother had lived at a comfortable home in London, as her father was a woolen mill manufacturer from Yorkshire. It was near a missionary college, whose students were often entertained in their home. No doubt, that influenced her toward a missionary vocation. Under this influence, and never forgetting the poverty and religious superstition of the Galician peasants from her time recuperating there, she decided four years later, at twenty-two, to give her life to becoming a missionary. She went to Pontevedra and lived with a senior single lady missionary. Some years later, she moved to be with another older, single English lady at Piedralaves, near Avila—Rachael Chesterman, in the Sierra de Gredos Mountains.

Their ministry with the local youth flourished. Alarmed, the local priest (with the support of the local doctor and mayor)

incited youths to stone them out of the village, with them
sheltering on the flank of their donkeys as they fled. Two young
missionaries from Madrid were dispatched to rescue them, one
being my father, escorting them on donkeys back through ninety-
five kilometers of trails through fir forests to Madrid. The next
year, Father and Mother were married in a blacksmith's shop in
Madrid. Shortly thereafter, they were on their way to Albacete.

My daughters and I visited that little town of Piedralaves,
meaning "the washing stones," with its mountain river still
flowing through the pueblo. The river bridge, as we discovered,
was a Roman bridge built in the second century BC. Beside it,
following a cut in the riverbank, we descended into an ancient
hostelry/pub that was still in use. To our astonishment, on the
wall were two faded photos, dated 1920, one of a young man on
his donkey and the other of the village center where my mother's
home had been! The photos clearly revealed the presence of my
parents there. Again, we marveled at the godly heritage we had
been given. Other photos, which we have received since that
trip, show summer conferences with the children of Piedralaves.
These were a regular summer event for missionaries in Madrid,
escaping from the hot city.

Our Departure for Edinburgh in 1930

With three births late in life, my mother had gynecological
problems that needed medical attention; it was time to retire
from the mission field. We were welcomed back into the home
of Father's elder sister and brother-in-law, who was an architect.
We stayed there some months before we had our first home. They
were lovely Christians, whose two daughters, Helen and Winnie
Ednie, remained staunch members of the Church of Scotland
all their lives. But other members of Father's family had strayed
from the faith, so we always felt estranged from them. Father
still lived the life of faith and began visiting Brethren assemblies

in German Switzerland and in Northern Germany. He became fluent in German, so he could preach regularly. At one point he had to squash a curious rumor that Hitler's mother was from the Brethren assemblies, so Hitler had to be a good man! Instead, Father clearly saw that he was evil. Father kept up this ministry until just before the outbreak of the war.

I arrived from Spain a sickly child with little initiative, in contrast to my sister Ethel, who was very much her father's daughter and full of it! When I was twelve and Ethel was ten, kindly friends of my father lived in North and South Shields, two small towns on the mouth of the Tyne River. Only a ferry connected the towns. Both couples were childless, and so they didn't understand (or perhaps didn't know) the feelings of children. I was sent to stay with the couple in North Shields, while my sister was separated across the river in South Shields. We were told we would not see each other, which we thought was an outrage, when we were so close to each other. Ethel took her revenge very quickly, waiting until her hostess was in the outside lavatory. Immediately, she bolted the door on the outside, leaving the inmate clamoring for quite a long time: "Let me out, let me out!" Eventually a neighbor heard the cries and rescued the lady. That was the end of a well-intentioned holiday!

Reflecting now, I wonder whether that first use of an outhouse gave me a childhood infection—for soon after, I had a serious attack of diphtheria and nearly died. I still remember a kindly nurse singing to me a popular song "Sunny Jim," which certainly was not "miserable me!" I was given lots of ice cream to ease my feverish throat, so I don't remember it as a bad experience—although the serum injected to deal with the diphtheria left me with a weak heart. I could not play sports, remained a sickly child, and developed swollen glands when I was thirteen. My father belonged to a generation that believed in homeopathy, and pills were prescribed for everything. When my swollen glands persisted, the alternative treatment was to go to the swimming baths where we now lived, at Portobello, a seaside suburb of Edinburgh. Sitting outside in a ring with others, wearing goggles, we spent two hours every afternoon getting ultra-violet ray treatment. It was a waste of time.

Although our church fellowship in Edinburgh was very conservative, there was an outreach to the social problems around us. I was fifteen or sixteen when I began to visit a local prison for a Sunday evening service behind bars. We would invite the prisoners to choose their favorite hymns. But one hymn became so constantly demanded that the prison chaplain advised us to stop this practice, for the audience always requested "Free from the law, O happy Condition!"

Looking back, I now see that a ministry to prisoners began long before I got involved with Chuck Colson in prison ministry. I realize it is valuable for teenagers to visit poor children also, whether in the Caribbean (as one of my grandsons did in Trinidad), or in Africa (as a granddaughter has done). It promotes compassion as an important education for later life. As Kierkegaard says, we learn retrospectively from the past, how to travel into the future.

At sixteen, having been allowed no exercise because of my heart condition, I was now two years behind my contemporaries at school, feeling "the dunce of the class" and often called "fatty."

Father, being from the land of Don Quixote, tried out a quixotic educational experiment with Ethel and myself. She was to jump two years ahead at her school, and I was to go to a cram college, Skerry's—for underprivileged adults—and jump three years ahead. She entered the University of Edinburgh at sixteen, and I joined her at seventeen. Louie entered the university two years later, but as the youngest, she was never as close to me as Ethel. But here our emotional paths all diverged again. University gave Ethel enormous confidence for the rest of her life, as well as two medals in jurisprudence and in constitutional law. Louie had to compete with us both. As soon Ethel graduated from the

University of Edinburgh, she was recruited to be a code-breaker in Hut Six at Bletchley Park, within the Enigma Program.

Later, she became one of the first Scottish women to become a solicitor on Royal Commissions, the first woman CEO of a major corporation, and was decorated by the Queen with the Order of the British Empire. Louie joined the civil service and later made the mistake to follow Ethel into the legal profession. She was very competent and became a lecturer at Dundee University on oil legislation for the development of the North Sea. But she was always in the shadow of Ethel, and tragically became an alcoholic in mid-life. The more Ethel tried to help her, the worse the drink problem intensified, until Louie died of the affliction. Much as she loved me, I was far away with my family in Oxford.

Meanwhile, my own hidden emotions were a total contrast to Ethel's confidence. I thought that by going to university a year before I should have done, under the crash program at Skerry's College, I had cheated the educational system. But instead of elation, I felt I was bogus, like "wallpaper"—constantly apologizing for breathing some of peoples' oxygen supply. My very existence became an apology, with an extremely low self-image. Here, later, Rita's strength was to give me new confidence after our marriage. For even though I graduated from Edinburgh University as the gold medallist of the Royal Geographical Society—as the best geography student in Scotland for that year—and was awarded a research fellowship, I was still bogus! Even later, when I went to Oxford with a scholarship to start doing my doctoral program after working as a regional planning officer in Scotland, I continued to feel bogus. These negative feelings lasted for twenty years—yet strangely, they were not crippling. Rather, they proved challenging.

Chapter Two

MEMOIRS OF THE
SECOND WORLD WAR

*W*e had moved from Edinburgh to the suburban seaside resort of Portobello in the early 1930s. I vividly remember lying in bed and seeing a huge monster in the sky. I rushed to the window to see the Graf Zeppelin floating by! In those days, it was an extraordinary technological feat to build an air balloon on such a vast scale. On reflection, it might have been a warning by the Nazis that they were now a world power, to be feared by the British. It had a political intent that we were innocent about, as war clouds began gathering.

Later we moved to another house, closer to the beach, in an area called East Brighton Crescent. West and East Brighton Crescents had been designed for naval veterans after the Battle of Trafalgar. They were an imitation of the kind of Georgian Circle at Bath, reproduced in Scotland. In late August 1939, the heavy cruiser HMS Edinburgh sailed into the Firth of Forth, ready to use its guns if the Germans tried to destroy the Forth Bridge, the vital north-south connection in eastern Scotland. To bomb it would be to disrupt communications on a vital artery between England and Scotland. The chief navigation officer on board was a friend of my father's, and when he visited our home in his uniform, I was much impressed—but he said nothing about what lay ahead. War was declared a week later, on September 2, and the next morning, the first air raid began. I was in my bedroom when a shrieking German bomber thundered overhead, flying at roof level to avoid the artillery guns; it was being chased by a small British Spitfire, machine guns rattling. On a neighboring wall, a man was washing his windows on a ladder; I saw him fall, hit by a stray bullet. I don't know whether it killed or simply wounded him, but my immediate reaction as a boy of sixteen was that the war was going to be "fun." Little did I know what was to follow.

But my father was to witness war's grim reality. Risking his own life, he frequently visited London to give comfort to small Christian communities when they were being bombed and suffering sleepless nights in air raid shelters built in their gardens, or herded together in the London Underground on rail platforms. We were all trained to wear gas masks, in case the Nazis used mustard gas. The war came to the nation with great force, unimaginable according to our previous experiences.

War Memoirs as a Student

The government decreed that those who entered a university would be allowed to finish a first degree and then be recruited for the war effort. Students like me, medically unfit, would be employed otherwise. I started at Edinburgh University in September 1941, and geography professor Ogilvie was particularly memorable. In his first lecture, he predicted what the world's trouble spots would be at the end of the twentieth century (he did not live to see his prediction come true): again it would be the Balkans; the whole Middle East; the Southern Russian Republics; and the Republics of Western China. Professor Ogilvie understood the power of ethnic minorities to rebel. He invited a few of us to volunteer for a noncurricular course in aerial photo interpretation, and I took it.

Unbeknownst to us all, Professor Ogilvie had been a spy in the Balkans during the First World War, and he was supplying RAF Intelligence with recruits, to join the war in the Western Mediterranean. In January 1944, just a few months before the end of my training for an M.A. hons. in Geography, I was summoned to Naval Intelligence headquarters in London. I was rejected for service because of my medical record, which deeply disappointed me, but my professor assured me I was fortunate. I now finished my degree, and immediately, I was recruited for "war work."

I had done a little "war work" already, as an undergraduate. We were allowed to volunteer three nights a week at the university, ready to go up onto the roof and remove any incendiary bombs that had landed there. It meant having great discussions with the others on duty in our warm room until the air raid warning sounded, then putting on helmets and climbing onto the open rooftops, ready to clear off any burning bombs with a bucket of sand and a spade. Incendiary bombs were used by the advanced Nazi fighters, to create a path of light for the following bombers to attack the shipyards of the Lower Clyde Valley.

God's Use of Others in "War Work"

Among my colleagues were James Torrance and John Hick, who as theological students debated vigorously. James and I were already beginning to sense that John Hick was becoming a heretic. James Barr debated here too; Torrance and I felt Barr was already becoming more "liberal," and he later became apostate in his advocacy of comparative religion. Meanwhile James and I began to ponder more deeply into the mystery of the Trinity, as expressive of the uniqueness of God.

Although I only knew him later, Dr. Martyn Lloyd-Jones was assistant to Lord Horder, the King's Physician, in Harley Street, London. As a Welsh Congregationalist, he did his "war work" as pulpit supply each weekend, traveling to chapels in Wales. Lacking a theological education, he read the Puritans so he could reuse their sermons for his own preaching. He was one of a group in the Cotswolds who revived Puritan theology. After the war, he founded Westminster Chapel and left his distinguished medical profession behind. His surrogate "spiritual son," Jim (J. I.) Packer, has been my lifelong friend since 1946.

Another academic doing "war work" was C. S. Lewis. Wounded in the World War I Battle of the Somme, he was exempt from military service in the Second World War, but the BBC took notice of him; his book *The Problem of Pain* was written in 1940 to encourage bombed refugees during the Battle of Britain. Britain still was religious enough to see the cause against the Nazis as a crusade against evil. One of his graduates, RAF Chaplain Stuart Barton Babbage, gently urged him to visit airfields on weekends and preach on Sunday mornings. At first, Lewis protested vehemently. He was not a chaplain, had never preached a sermon in his life, had not studied theology, etc. "Oh, Lewis, you must do your 'war work' in boosting the morale of the pilots." Lewis gave five series of broadcast talks, later published in five booklets and eventually collated into his famous book, *Mere Christianity*.

After the war, RAF Chaplain Babbage returned to Australia. There, he was appointed Canon of Sydney Cathedral, activated to educate lay Christians. Much later, he visited Regent College during its first summer school, to encourage our similar venture. In 2004, he humorously titled his own book *Memoirs of a Loose Canon*.

Post-War Disenchantment

Immediately after I graduated in the summer of 1944, I was recruited to the StrathClyde Valley Regional Planning Authority in Glasgow. There I served for the next eighteen months. Our job was to plan a new town east of the city at East Kilbride, to house people from the bombed areas of StrathClyde, just as the Greater London Plan was set up to build new towns around the suburbs of London, for those who had lost their homes in air raids there. I was the first geographer to be appointed; all my colleagues were architects, in addition to one engineer. My assignments were to survey the location for the new town, to survey the boundaries of the first national park in Scotland (around Loch Lomond), and to relocate sewage outfalls for the Ayrshire coastal towns, discharging into the Firth of Clyde. But in reality, such locations were political decisions made by the municipalities. I quickly grew disenchanted with regional planning, which I left as soon as the war was over.

Chapter Three

DOCTORATE STUDIES
AT OXFORD

*O*n my graduation in 1944, besides the Gold Medal of the
Royal Scottish Geographical Society, I received the Shaw
McFie Lang Fellowship, which enabled me to go to Oxford—a
dream that I had never thought possible. But first, I had to write
a BSc thesis on the cultural contrast between the Scottish and
English sides of the Solway Firth Plain. I did this in one year, but
almost immediately, I became disenchanted with this as well; the
School of Geography at Oxford had been the headquarters for
Naval Intelligence, and my senior colleagues had been turning
out guidebooks for naval commanders in the countries that they
were visiting. It was all very factual. Now, they had to redesign
the field of academic geography and what it might become. I
turned in another direction, choosing as my doctoral thesis
a specialized topic of sixteenth-century Spain, based on the
Archives of the Indies in Seville and the Archives in Valencia.
Essentially, I switched my doctoral program to research in
"the history of ideas." It was a study of cultural transmission—
essentially, the exchanges of plants—between the Aztecs of the
New World and the Arab cultivators who developed the *huertas,*
irrigated gardens, of the Levante coast in the east of Spain during

the mid-sixteenth through early seventeenth centuries. These were the two leading horticultural civilizations of the world at that time. Ever since, I have essentially followed this new trajectory, the history of ideas. My Spanish studies later helped me to broaden others' horizons, in the shift I advocated from teaching "systematic theology" toward the introduction among evangelicals of "spiritual theology," including doing receptive exegesis with my colleague Bruce Waltke in our cooperative studies on the psalms.

Having grown up in Spain, it felt natural to do research there, and I visited Spain for my research shortly after the Spanish Civil War ended. My Spanish tutor in Oxford was Professor of Spanish Literature Salvador de Madariaga, who had been the Spanish ambassador to the League of Nations after the First World War. It had been President Woodrow Wilson's vision that the League of Nations would represent the different ethnic and cultural communities of the world. Therefore, each ambassador should be a humanist philosopher. Wilson believed that the world needed ambassadors acting like Greek philosophers, to represent the ethnic diversities of the nations; i.e., government and diplomacy by humanists. It was a great dream but, like the League itself, all too utopian.

Salvador de Madariaga had escaped from the Civil War but had fallen out of touch with old friends. He asked me to act as a courier to help him reconnect with the rector of the University of Madrid and others. I was also put in touch with a famous painter of that day, Pio Baroja, and his nephew—who was an anthropologist—as a guest in their summer home in the Basque Mountains. I was further invited to the first Quaternary Congress, consisting of specialists in the Pleistocene period (geomorphologists, glaciologists, and primitive art historians), to visit the prehistoric paintings in the Cantabrian Mountains, which only recently became so useful for researching human evolution.

Returning to Oxford, I found it a stimulating environment in ways I had never imagined, given my religious upbringing. My mother was considered "open-minded"; she came from the "Open" Brethren. However, my father came from the "Glanton" Brethren, an offshoot of the "London" or "Tight" Brethren. There had been, then, some tensions between my parents. I had always navigated between them, feeling much more sympathetic to my mother. This prepared me to be "blown wide open" later, as I experienced living with the head of the Orthodox Church in Britain.

The Glanton party did, at least, believe that each community should be free to settle their own internal disputes, whereas the London party controlled all disputes from their headquarters in London, which later became a one-man dictatorship. One of our local disputes occurred when I was sixteen, sitting in a business meeting for two hours of intense argument. I spent that night in tears and never forgot the experience. It felt so wrong for Christians to have such quarrels. In truth, it drew me closer to my mother's side of the debate.

Another ridiculous event occurred the first Sunday I arrived in Oxford. A friend of my father was very concerned that I would worship in "the right assembly." He had given me a moped so I could ride sixty miles from Oxford into the heart of the Cotswolds, where there was a "right place of worship." I set off on a snowy day, but the engine seized up, leaving me stranded in a small village with no church, and no bus back to Oxford until the evening. I had to keep warm in the local pub. This gave me plenty of time to determine that the following Sunday, I would go to an "Open Assembly," even though I was still afraid that it might be the seat of Satan! Instead, I discovered a community of very kindly Christians, enjoying a lovely, simple spirit of worship.

Meanwhile, I met my companion in our lodgings: Donald Wiseman (1918–2010), formerly a Group Captain in the RAF and the Chief Intelligence officer for Mediterranean forces in the

Second World War. Having been awarded an OBE with military decorations, he was returning to finish his Master's degree in Assyriology at Wadham College. He was a member of the Open Brethren. Don taught me the phrase, "keep looking up," which I still use to encourage others. He became Professor of Assyriology at the University of London, and Keeper of Assyriology at the British Museum. He pioneered a new thread of Old Testament studies, emphasizing they needed to be interpreted in the context of the history of the ancient civilizations of the Middle East.

The following year, Don moved into Wadham College and I needed new accommodation. One of my senior colleagues at the School of Geography had a friend, the Orthodox Dr. Nicholas Zernov (1898–1980), who was looking for a tenant to share his apartment at 27 Norham Road. His wife Melitza was a dentist in London, and on weekends either he returned there or she came to him. I resided seven years with him. He taught me the reasoning behind the importance of icons: learning to see the whole world as symbolic of the ever-deepening mysteries of creation. As professor of Russian history, he introduced me to the Russian mystics and philosophers, about whom he was writing books. He was one of the founders of the ecumenical Society of St. Albans and St. Sergius. He gave me, through the Russian term *staretz*, a new understanding of spiritual friendship. Through the thin wall between our bedrooms, I could hear him every morning, praying urgently and lovingly with God. I had no prayer life like that. He began to impress and inspire me with his piety.

Nicholas gathered a group of University Dons who were Christians for dinner once a month, so I became included, although none of them were "evangelical" in my old way of thinking. Basil Mitchell (1917–2011), an ecumenical Anglican, was a philosopher of religion. Professor D'Antrev, Serena Professor of Italian, was, like C. S. Lewis, a fellow of Magdalen College. Lewis (1898–1963), meanwhile, was vigorously critiquing D'Antrev's views of natural law! There was also the librarian of the University Library, and his wife, Mrs. Southern, the President of Lady Margaret Hall. Unlike the famous "Inklings," this group did not review much of each other's writings. They just met for convivial gatherings.

Romance and Marriage

I lived in a generation that presumed that anyone who was serious about their profession would not get married until finished with their professional training. Today, one gets into marriage whether or not one has money—but to be honorable in that culture, I would not offer my hand to a lady until I felt sure I could provide for her with a stable job. She would not be expected to work outside of our home, and hopefully, I would also be able to provide the down payment for a house, so that I could offer her a home to live in. It was a very different culture from the one we live in today, and I was twenty-nine or thirty years old before I started thinking of marriage.

Ethel, my sister, always had a lot of friends back in Edinburgh. In 1952, I invited her to accompany me through Spain, to visit our parents' missionary friends in Madrid. She then would leave me in Tangier while I pursued my research in North Africa for three months. I had been awarded a research grant by the Royal Geographic Society, to map, identify, and classify the different kinds of indigenous irrigation across North Africa, from Morocco to Tunisia. I only wanted to be with Ethel, but she said, "Oh no, I have a friend and I think she would love to come with us." I just thought *That's Ethel again, manipulating my invitations*, as she had done on other occasions. The friend she brought this time was Rita Davidson. Rita's family lived in a Glasgow suburb, Bearsden, but she was teaching in a private boys' school in Edinburgh, where she and Ethel had become friends. Reluctantly, I agreed that Rita could accompany us—whereas she thought the rest of our family was also going! The two girls planned to spend a weekend in Paris before meeting me at my ferry boat train. We would be coming in at different stations, and we all thought we understood the arrangement.

But it had been a tense weekend for the two girls. Ethel, a solicitor, had wanted to spend time at the Law Court, while Rita—as a tourist visiting Paris for the first time—wanted to see the Eiffel Tower! When I arrived, I waited all day for them at my arrival station. Meanwhile, they did the same at their station. When we eventually met up that evening, at the train station for our joint departure on the night train for Madrid, we were all in a very bad mood. I explained, given our separately arranged bookings, that we would be only somewhere on the same train. However, we quickly found we were in the same carriage—then in the same compartment—and then, to my amazement, I found myself sitting exactly opposite Rita. Meanwhile, I had had a strange premonition: this mysterious lady might become my wife.

Things did happen very quickly after that. By the time they were preparing to embark from Gibraltar and sail home, and I to proceed through North Africa, Rita and I were very attracted to each other. I visited Rita's family just before term began, and again at Christmas, when we announced our engagement! I had bought the ring that Rita wanted: an emerald in the middle and two diamonds on the sides, to symbolize Christ at the center of our lives, with a diamond on either side (so it was, for sixty-three years of married life!). Once a week, we would phone, with many letters in between. Near our wedding on March 20, 1953, Rita wrote: "Oh, Jim, I don't think I have enough love for us to get married." I said, "That's no problem, my dear, I've got love for both of us!" We were married in the chapel of Glasgow University.

Years later, our children continued to marvel however we had got married to each other, so different were we, as "chalk and cheese!" Yet it provided a freedom for each child also to be so different from each other.

Chapter Four

EXPANDING HORIZONS AT OXFORD THROUGH NEW FRIENDSHIPS

*I*n the spring of 1953, at the time when C. S. Lewis was preparing to take up an appointment as full Professor of Literature in Cambridge, and as I was preparing to get married—moving out from the joint accommodation—I asked Lewis what had been his central message in his Christian writings. "All my writings," he said, "are against reductionism ... this is contained in the three lectures that I gave to the Department of Education at the University of Newcastle, 'On the Abolition of Man.'" He spoke—and wrote—about people having "flat chests," meaning that thinkers who were secularists had no awareness of the eternal or spiritual dimension of man. He had written an angry review of a book by two young Australian critics of literature, trying to reduce literary criticism to "a new science." In the same conversation, I told him, "I'm fascinated by the new novel you have just published, *Till We Have Faces*." He responded, "I'm very disappointed, because the publisher has refused to allow more than 1,000 copies to be printed, since there were no sales for this book." Ten years later, when Lewis died, there still had been no further printing. Yet Lewis told me it was the best book he had ever written. It would take another generation to appreciate what Lewis had been trying to communicate.

Lewis was not alone in his literary fight against reductionism. Another member of our Saturday evening dinner group, Marjorie Reeves (1905–2005), was a literary scholar making the same protest as a devout Christian. Also in Oxford, there was a debate among philosophers of logical positivism, led by A. J. Ayers.

The only other relationship I had with Lewis was in the Socratic Club—and it was tangential, for Lewis was a shy man, never revealing his inner emotions, not even to Tolkien and the other members of the Inklings. The Socratic club came to be at the behest of Stella Aldwinckle, on the staff of St. Aldates Church. Stella was quite eccentric; she lived with her horse in a hut on Port Meadows, the Common land on the flood plain of the Evenlode. Stella had heard the complaint of a woman student at Somerville College (itself somewhat hostile to Christianity) that there was no place where Christian women students could discuss theology. Stella took up their cause and began holding Socratic Club meetings on Monday evenings at St. Hilda's College, then at St. Aldates Church on Thursdays. It was like a second debating society, but for Christianity instead of politics. C. S. Lewis was invited to assist, which as an Irishman, he did with great gusto. On one memorable evening, the Fellow in Philosophy at Somerville, G. E. M. Anscombe (1946–1970), herself a strong Catholic, challenged him on his explanation of miracles, on which he had published a book. He was publicly defeated, and he revised a section of the book in its next edition. Later, another woman, Edith Starkie, professor of German, ran a campaign against his election to the chair in poetry, which was another defeat! These early women dons had to be strong women, as it was only in 1959 that the women's colleges were given full collegiate authority.

Two doors away from where I lived, and peripheral to Dr.
Zernov's group, was Michael Polanyi (1891–1976), a neighbor
I occasionally greeted. He impressed me as shy, a chemist—not
in the circles of humanists I was more familiar with—and living
as an exile, for he was a Jewish refugee from Hungary who had
been elected a Fellow of Merton College. His colleagues expected
he would achieve the Nobel Prize in chemistry. Instead, his son
obtained it years later. For he was diverted by the ideological
fight against the Soviet aetiology of biology, which began in the
early 1930s with the ideology of communism. As a true scientist,
Polanyi protested that science is not based on presuppositions,
but free to full inquiry, as evidence dictates. Likewise, he taught
that the observer is not an abstraction, but a person with moral
obligations to be truthful. All this he summarized in his book
Personal Knowledge (1950). He too was against reductionism,
writing another book, *The Tacit Dimension*, but I don't know if
C. S. Lewis ever knew of his works. Regrettably, it was only later
that I became immensely influenced by his way of thinking,
for he left for Manchester in 1948. There, he occupied a chair
in the sociology of knowledge. He got to know the systematic
theologian Tom Torrance (Thomas F. Torrance, 1913–2003),
whose sister had married the Astronomer Royal in Manchester,
Sir Bernard Lovell (1913–2012), and who was beginning to
explore the new field of astrophysics. In turn, Tom Torrance was
influenced by Lovell, his brother-in-law, as well as by Polanyi, to
write his own *Science of Theology*. Since I was a family friend of
the Torrances through my sister, who was their family solicitor
in Edinburgh, Tom became very supportive of me, even giving
me his lecture notes and essays at the beginning of my new
life at Regent much later. In 1982, his younger brother James
(James B. Torrance, 1923–2003), my old Edinburgh colleague,
addressed the British Council of Churches, saying that we should
not practice a dysfunctional theology, biased either towards the
charismatic focus of the Pentecostals on the Holy Spirit, nor that

of the evangelicals upon Christ, nor that of the old liberals on the Fatherhood of God, but a renewed Trinitarian theology.

Although I lived a few yards opposite the entrance to Tolkien's home (J. R. R. Tolkien, 1892–1973) in Catte Lane, I never met him personally. But I was a colleague of his younger son, Christopher, at St. Catherine's College. I also met Hugo Dyson, who famously walked around the grounds of Magdalen College in 1933, until 3 a.m., the same time when C. S. Lewis was "reluctantly converted." A colleague of Tolkien at Merton College, Dyson was vivacious and transparent in faith, whereas as a sacramental Catholic, Tolkien never openly shared his faith, even with his sons. He found the public openness of Lewis's faith embarrassing. Lewis and Tolkien, later mutual friends, had both been wounded at the Battle of the Somme in 1916, as was John MacMurray (1891–1976), a fellow of Balliol College.

Another exemplar was Martyn Lloyd-Jones (1899–1981), whom I knew through his daughter Elizabeth at Somerville college, and whom I mentioned earlier.

The center of Oxford, with its multiple colleges, is a small community. Therefore I enjoyed the benefit of having lunch almost every week with one or two friends at the university cafeteria, which was among the science buildings near Keble College. One of my close friends was John Houghton (b. 1931), fellow of stratospheric physics at Jesus College. With the initial support of the Master of St. Peter's Hall, Canon J. P. Thornton-Duesbery (1902–1985), we negotiated the financial support of the British Council to establish a hostel for overseas students, especially the Russians. This is still thriving on Banbury Road. John Houghton went on to become Director General of Weather Forecasting, then Co-Chairman of the International Panel of Climate Change (IPCC), was knighted, and was awarded the Nobel Prize along with his colleagues and US Vice-President Al Gore.

Another Oxford colleague, Max Cowan (1931–2002), was a South African physical anthropologist and brain anatomist, who later helped us as an elder of Northway Chapel. He preached eloquently yet modestly, and his wife and sister-in-law started a Sunday school. Sadly, he abandoned his faith later in the United States, where eventually he became founder of the *Journal of Neuroscience*, as a distinguished pioneer of the new science of brain circuitry.

John S. Grinalds (b. 1938), Rhodes scholar at Brasenose College, was not yet a Christian while at Oxford, yet his wife was devout, and I often spoke to him about my faith. Years later, I learned that his commander at West Point Military Academy had also tried to persuade him to accept Christ as his Lord. But it was in a foxhole in Vietnam that he became a Christian, and he, in turn, led his junior officer, Oliver North, to Christ. I will say more about John Grinalds in a later chapter.

Chapter Five

MARRIAGE AND
FAMILY LIFE AT OXFORD

Our First Year

*W*hen Rita and I were first married, I arranged to rent
an apartment in Bardwell Road, a block from where
I had lived for seven years with Nicholas Zernov. For our first
Christmas, Rita was anxious to entertain. She was a simple
cook, but she made up for that with elaborate table decorations.
She designed the table with a Christmas scene, including lots
of cotton wool to imitate snow. Delighted that it looked so
beautiful, she lit a candle—which tipped over, setting the whole
table ablaze! In a panic, she turned on the fire extinguisher. The
flames went out, but now the table was badly charred. It seemed
that it would be impossible to eat at that table that evening with
our eight guests. Still in panic, she rushed out on her bicycle and
came around to the School of Geography where I was having a
tutorial, listening to a student reading his essay. She burst into
my room, explained, and very calmly I apologized that we would
have to postpone the tutorial "because my wife says the house is
on fire." I rushed back following her, also bicycling. Upon arrival
I found a black tarry substance all over the table and smoke
still filling the home, so we had to open up all the windows. I

said, "Oh my dear, this is no problem. We have a large piece of plywood. Let's put it on the table and cover it all up. Then we will get another tablecloth, and we'll have the meal just as if nothing ever happened." I put her to bed to rest from all the panic, set the table, and finished the cooking. When the guests arrived, we didn't tell them anything that had happened. But that was our first scenario of entertainment. It came with a burst of flames.

Our Second Year

Our apartment was not large enough for children, but the day following our first anniversary, Rita gave birth to our son. As Christopher was to repeat many times later, "The day after my Daddy and Mummy got married I was born!" It has helped me to remember these anniversaries! But it meant we needed to buy a house. The first big decision we faced was whether to go for the cheaper municipal rate at 2 percent, or should we choose the fixed rate of 3½ percent? We decided on the latter, which later saved us a lot of money as rates increased.

Founding a New Chapel

With a few friends, such as Max Cowan, we decided that we would start a new church. I was quite happy in the church we were attending, but increasingly we wanted something that was more interdenominational. Max's wife and sister had already started a Sunday School on the Headley housing estate, on the northwest side of the city. We all were heavily mortgaged with our homes, but in our idealism, four or five of us also mortgaged for the church. Along with a grant from a kind friend, Sir John Laing, we built Northway Chapel. I had wanted to have the church in Oxford, to be close to the students' colleges, but this was not practically possible. Most of the land in the city were on leaseholds to rich colleges such as St. John's.

Since we were only a small group, we needed the support of Christian students—both to attend and to help us with the singing. Since they would miss out on lunch in college, we promised we would give them lunch at home with us. They cycled five miles to our home, or else got a ride in our overloaded car. Rita would spend all Saturday evening making soup for Sunday lunch. Our children scouted around during the services to recruit our lunch guests. Our table was small, so we extended it with plywood from a ping-pong table, all covered with a nice white tablecloth, to seat sixteen or eighteen.

These lunches were memorable. Two regular students were brothers: David Alexander, who later created Lion Publishing, and Dennis Alexander, later a missionary professor of biology at the American University of Beirut, and even later Professor of Science and Faith at Cambridge. They were nephews of A. J. P. Taylor, a political scientist at Magdalen College and colleague of C. S. Lewis. We heard the rumor that, as an agnostic, Taylor could not stand Lewis, who was so open about his faith. "Oh, no," was their report. "It was simply that breakfast at high table was a silent meal, because of headaches from the drinking the night before. Lewis broke the rule by talking too much!" In fact, Taylor was very tolerant about Lewis's faith, for his own wife had grown up in a Plymouth Brethren family.

Our Sunday lunches were "operation family—all hands on deck." Little did we know how each of our family would be shaped by hospitality, as a way of life. For all the children helped us on Saturday afternoons to prepare the Sunday lunch, as they too recruited the students for the meal. I would then often go out on a walk with students, to chat more informally in the countryside. It was a habit of walking and mentoring that I continued throughout latter years. But Claire reminds me that on one occasion, a couple stayed behind on the couch, where he proposed marriage to her. Penny and Claire were hiding behind the couch, startling them by being the first to congratulate them on their engagements. Many times, when the table had its full capacity of twenty-four, delegated to a side table, the two sisters would crawl under the table and quietly tie together the shoe laces of some guest, without being caught!

Two other students we entertained on Sundays were from the Czech and Slovakian Republics. One from the latter was named Dalibor; he already had his doctorate from Moscow in nuclear physics and was in Oxford as a post-doctoral student. In Bratislava, Slovakia, he had attended a Moravian Brethren church. His real reason for attending Oxford was inspiring: after his lab work was finished each evening, he would consult modern translations of the Bible so that he could translate John's Gospel into Slovakian, to take home to his people. We arranged the printing, and when he did return—with a small group of Christian philosophers at Oxford, who had opened a secret smuggling service of Bibles into Czechoslovakia—Dalibor's *John's Gospel* was smuggled too! Later, we paid a memorable visit to him at his home church, by which time he was President of the Slovakian Federation of Scientists, and we embraced with tears of joy.

With Dalibor in Oxford, there was a young Czech student writing his thesis on Bonhoeffer; he expected to be martyred like Bonhoeffer when he returned to Prague. In 1980, a group of philosophers in Oxford created an educational foundation as an underground movement, to teach in Prague and smuggle Bibles into Czechoslovakia. This became the Jan Hus Institute, and it was supported by the first President of the Czech Republic after the fall of communism.

Dalibor and his Czech companion inspired me with their dedication. Just as they were willing to lay down their lives for Christ, I should be prepared to give up everything—not concerned about my profession, but ready to give my life for Christ, in the way they were exemplifying. God was already preparing us, as a family, to leave Oxford years later.

At our luncheon table,we had another Czech student, an economist. She had been sent to Oxford to do a doctorate in economic planning, for their National Institute of Planning. Years later, we met her in Bratislava. She had become a Christian, and now was secretary to the bishop! "How did you become a Christian?" we asked. "It was just sitting at your Sunday luncheons," she replied, "listening to the conversations and seeing the new spirit of hospitality. I had never seen that before."

Viktor Kis: Protected by the Armor of Light

Another inspiring visitor to our home in about 1965 was Professor Viktor Kis, head of the Department of Anatomy in the University of Budapest. He visited Oxford by invitation of my colleague Le Gros Clark. Over a meal, I asked him, however had he survived, as one of five national leaders of the evangelical churches of Hungary, through the Nazi and then the Soviet occupation of his country? His cryptic response was "just putting on the armor of light." Then he elaborated on how he was so guarded. "I plan to visit a town or city to give a Christian address, so I inform the KGB agency in Budapest. I inform them of my time of arrival, the location of the meeting, and enclose a copy of my address. They have all the information about my movements and public speeches." It was all about transparency, the antithesis of how lovers of darkness dwell in darkness. On one sad occasion, two of the other denominational leaders turned up at the office of the agency that supplied them with printing paper for their publishing needs, saying the others did not need their quota for the next year; it was a lie. The KGB doubled their surveillance on them, arguing logically that "if these two deceive and are treacherous to their own associates, by how much more are they trying to trick us!" The KGB was right. These two were dismissed as reputable Christian leaders.

I have discovered since then that in the bureaucratic mind-set of religious institutions, people find it very hard to remain transparent—as we all find personally, if we are insecure personalities who wear a mask and do not show a face. Professor Kis was lion-hearted indeed, with great and inspiring courage.

Third Acre Rise and Family Dedications

It took courage for my father to visit our Northway Church, and he came just once—a week before he suddenly died. What upset him most was that we had a small organ playing during worship. To him, our worship was in heaven, where no instruments were needed! The fact was that we were a small community, who could not sing loudly—yet we needed the folks outside to know we were having a service, to welcome them in. Even that did not change his mind! Yet I have always highly esteemed my father's faith. It is a very rich heritage for me.

Rita's father, who had died in 1952, had endowed Rita with 1,000 pounds sterling, towards the down payment for a home of our own. We found an ideal house on the west side of Oxford in a cul-de-sac, 17 Third Acre Rise. The houses were built on lots of a third of an acre, which would provide a safe place for the children to play.

We were blessed with four children. Christopher, our firstborn, was dedicated to the Lord at the home of Rita's mother, now a widow, in Thorntonhall, outside of Glasgow. Our three daughters were dedicated by "Uncle Melville"—Melville Capper, Professor of Surgery in Bristol. We were both trustees of Mueller's Homes in Bristol, and together we had started the Young Men's Bible Study conferences in Oxford. "Uncle" Melville had big surgical hands, skillful to heal, so tender toward little children. Claire still remembers him singing, "He has the whole world in His hands.... the tiny little children in His hands!"

Our Children's Early Education

On the top of Cumnor Hill Road, west of our cul-de-sac, there was a kindergarten—"Pooks"—where all our children started their education. Then they all went to the local primary school at Botley. From there, Christopher got a scholarship to attend New College School; Lydele and Claire likewise received scholarships to go to Oxford Girls High School, all very competitive. Lydele's scholarship covered all her expenses: lunches, transport, fees. At New College School, Christopher joined the boys' choir, giving him a lifetime love of music. But Penny sat her exam the summer we left for Canada, so she could not take advantage of her exam results.

Our next-door neighbor, Stanley Whitcomb, became another "uncle" to the children. He worked for Morris bicycles at Cowley, which later became Morris Motor Works. During the war, he had been a supervisor making ammunition in the factory. His garage was a great workshop for Christopher to explore and to learn about tools, of which I knew nothing. His wife died about 1963, so he also allowed the children to watch his television for one hour after school. He supported our way of education, even though we did not have a television set on principle.

Each of the children also explored other friendships. Christopher frequented a house out on the dangerous Cumnor Hill road, where four children lived: Lewis, Nora, Martin and Freddy. He was a particular friend of the two younger boys. The father was a famous scientist, Heinz London, a Jewish refugee from Nazi Germany. One afternoon when Christopher was there, Heinz came back very excited: as a pioneer in superconductivity, that day he had reached the lowest temperature ever recorded by man on Earth. Christopher never forgot the power of having a great and inquisitive scientific mind.

On the same dangerous hill lived another family, the Brainsmiths. Christopher's friend, Ian Brainsmith, had two younger sisters, Claire and Jill. One day, coming home from Pook school, Jill stepped off the sidewalk into the path of an oncoming car and was killed. She was only seven.

More often, our girls made friends within the cul-de-sac, and every day—then every Friday afternoon—they had tea with Mr. and Mrs. Robinson, across the cul-de-sac from us. Penny used to sit on Mr. Robinson's knees, and one day, the five-year-old innocently asked what he did for a living. Solemnly, the famous professor of philosophy answered, "Well, Penny, I think, and I think about my thinking when I teach, and I write about thinking." She looked at him with disgust. "Is that all you do?" Mr. and Mrs. Robinson had no children, and they loved the three girls coming to visit them. After tea, they would all play a card game.

While Lydele and Penny did more things together, Claire—our middle girl—had a mind of her own. She often visited a farm half a mile away and spent time with the Gees family, whose daughter Tussle played with her there on the farm.

There was one dramatic event that all the girls remember. One day, Penny—the youngest—did not come home from school. Alone in the house and very scared, Lydele phoned the police and told them that Penny was missing! They were afraid that she had been killed like the neighbor girl, Jill, so they even looked in the ditch—but there was no Penny there. Meanwhile, absentmindedly I had invited Penny to ride with me on my moped, to do some shopping in Oxford. In those days, there were no precautions about having helmets nor, indeed, against letting children stand on the front of the scooter. I regularly commuted to the university on my scooter, three miles away, and of course, we rode without any helmets. We also had no cell phones, so no one knew where Penny could be until I brought her home, safe and sound.

My daughters have also reminded me of a gentle revolt they held one day. At Northway Chapel, we had two Sunday morning services. Two of the girls—only nine and eleven at the time—decided one service was enough, so they asked, "Can we walk to church for the service?" We said they could, but it was over five miles away. They did this many times! Looking back, I think that we treated our children more like small adults compared with the present generation. Mercifully, they made the walk safely.

On Sunday afternoons, I was leader of the local Boy Crusader class in the city, while our daughters attended the girls' class. I had one memorable visit from Sir John Laing, the wealthy builder who donated our first funding to build Northway Chapel. By now, he was one of the most eminent businessmen in Britain, constructing airfields in wartime Britain, then creating the motorways. Later, he founded London Bible College. But most of all, he loved to visit the Crusader classes throughout Britain. He was truly a humble servant of God.

Lydele has reminded me that being high spirited, she did get into trouble at school. Girls who got into trouble were sent home with a letter from the headmistress, so that their parents would give the punitive treatment. But the headmistress, Mrs. Warnock, never sent me a letter, because I was the bursar of the college where her husband was the principal!

Looking back, our home life seemed idyllic—but I lived with tension in college life. As an elder at our church, I attended prayer meeting each Tuesday night—but it was also guest night at the college's high table. As college bursar, I was supposed to stay to hear my colleagues' criticism as to whether it was a good dinner. Then, I had to leave unceremoniously although the meal was scarcely finished. I rushed to the church—late—for the prayer meeting. Neither group understood my compromises.

Chapter Six

TEACHING AT OXFORD

Entering the Complexity
of Oxford's Tutorial System

I had been fortunate in that after the war, the University
was short-staffed. That was why, although still completing
my doctorate, I was appointed a University Lecturer in 1947.
Looking back, it was nightmarish: completing my BSc in one
year, traveling in Spain, completing the doctorate in two years,
and in my third year preparing lectures to teach at the School of
Geography. I have never worked so hard, ever since!

As I started teaching at Oxford, I began to specialize in the
interface between the physical landscape and the modifications
in the history of man, in changing them into cultural landscapes.
My training in air-photographic interpretation, and the RAF
archives at Benson airfield, outside Oxford, helped tremendously.
The unique "tutorial" system at Oxford also became a major part
of my life.

My children have sometimes complained that I have an
extended family beyond them—and they are right. Often, I paid
more attention to students than to my own family. Students
played a great role in my life, because their personal confidences

did much to enrich me concerning what Hannah Arendt was to call "the human condition." This particularly occurred within Oxford's tutorial system. In the Middle Ages, Oxford was a monastic institution, as revealed in some of the college names: All Souls, Christ Church, Jesus College. As teachers, we had two masters: we had a college appointment—as a lecturer, or a fellowship, or both—at other colleges; and there was also a University appointment as a lecturer or full professor. Still, the tutorial system remained central to Oxford education. Its emphasis was on the humanities—not the sciences, which Cambridge had adopted during the Edwardian period. Unlike other universities, attendance at lectures was voluntary, but the weekly tutorial was compulsory. A selection of essays was to be written as a strategy to prepare for the final examination. Often the lectures were on very specialized topics, reflective of the professors' lifetime research. In the intimacy of the tutorials, however, tutors and pupils often became lifelong friends. I kept a book of the addresses and annual news of many pupils, over many years. This intimacy of the classical *paedia* model of education created experiences both comic and tragic.

The Comedy of the Passing of "Divers"

First, then, comedy. In the immediate post-war years, students were still forced to write an exam on divinity, to indicate that they had some understanding of Christian heritage. This "Divers" exam took place before they could officially enter the university. My first college appointment in 1948, after being elected by the university the previous year, was as a lecturer of Brasenose College. Brasenose was very much a sports college, always hoping their college team would become the university team. A student who came to the notice of the authorities as not having passed his "Divers" exam was the captain of the college rugby team. The college fellows interviewed the failed candidate in

"Divers," allowing him one more chance by simply asking him one question: "Who was the first king of Israel?" Hesitantly, he blurted out, "King Saul!" Relieved that the future of college rugby was safe, they dismissed him with, "Quite right my boy, quite right." But at the exit, the candidate hesitantly turned and said, "But I should have added, Saul was afterwards called 'Paul.'" The practice of "Divers" collapsed shortly after that incident.

One of my Brasenose students was Colin Cowdray, a cricketer, who lasted just two years at Oxford (1952–1954). Truly, his only motive in being there was cricket. Eventually, as Lord Colin Cowdray (1932–2000) he became one of England's national sports heroes.

Comedy also occurred with those privileged students who never took their education seriously. One wealthy student from Toronto claimed the totem pole in his room gave him all the luck he needed to pass without effort! Being lazy, he was awarded a fourth class degree, a form of cliff-hanging success. Years later, I met him in Tangier in the consulate office. When I asked, "What are you doing here?" he replied, "I just killed an Arab in a car accident, so I am asking the Consul to bail me out!"

Another privileged student was Ponsonby, whose great-grandfather was Queen Victoria's private secretary. His predecessors were all courtiers at Buckingham Palace, treated almost as part of the royal family. I warned him he would be "sent down" if he did not do better work. "Oh sir," he said, "I have done better than any of my predecessors, for this is my second year at Oxford!"

Even the military provided comedy. Many of the students returning from the war, like my friend Don Wiseman, were senior officers. At Brasenose, one such was John S. Grinald (b. 1932), later Major General of the US Marines. He was the first marine to be awarded a Rhodes Scholarship, granted while he was at West Point. Holding a military post solo at an Oxford college, he could not leave for holidays. Being quite humorous, he liked to joke about the military bureaucracy.

Tragedies of Oxford's Intense Academic Life

However, the academic pressures of Oxford are often intense. One Hertford student from Florida was doing a research thesis under my supervision. Emotionally, he was fatherless. His parents had divorced, and he had seen too many women on his father's arm to have any trust in him, as he confided desperately. He asked, when my family was planning a camping holiday in France, for our address. I explained we would have none. I gave him plenty of work to do until we returned, but in our absence, he committed suicide.

Another college friend was Michael Foster (1903–1959), a famous Christian philosopher, tutor at Christ Church College and National Chairman of the Students Christian Movement. In 1959, we dined together in Brasenose on a Thursday evening, but he did not share his deep loneliness and depression with me. The next Thursday, he put his head in a gas oven and died. He had brilliantly explored ontology for the evidence of God, but his own depression proved too much.

A third tragedy concerned a young friend, Pixie, who came to me one October to ask about the meaning of baptism, and how she could be baptized. She was going on a cruise with her parents in November, so we planned to have her baptized on her return. Her mother, like her, was a lovely Christian, but I knew her father was fraudulent in his so-called "faith" and had betrayed his wife. Pixie must have suddenly discovered this. On their cruise through the Baltic, she disappeared overboard. She had a baptism of death.

Made hypersensitive to those in depression, I still mourn such tragic deaths.

One of the most moving events among my colleagues at Hertford was the death of a young Fellow. We had been to his funeral, so we were very solemn at the high table that evening. Sir Wilfred Le Gros Clark was our esteemed and internationally famous professor of anatomy. He had researched the forgery of the "Piltdown man," discovered in the chalk of the English Downs and supposed to be the most ancient evidence of a human in England. Leaning across the table that evening, he startled us all with his question to me: "Jim, do you believe in the resurrection?" It was taboo at dinner to ever talk about sex or religion. In my shyness, I blurted out, "It is inconceivable, for me, not to believe in the resurrection." He responded, "I too believe in the resurrection." Our cynical, secular science colleagues murmured it must be rather wonderful to believe in the resurrection, indicating what high eminence can do!

Later, when we were leaving for Canada, LeGros Clark gave me as a parting gift a book, *The Ulysses Factor,* saying: "Jim, I don't know what you're doing, but your motive must be like Ulysses's!"—for the book describes how explorers go beyond the horizons and explore new territories of the mind and spirit. I was taking a little family across the oceans to little-known Vancouver, to do a new thing. It was a great compliment, very encouraging to us in the years ahead, that Sir Wilfred had cheered me on in this way.

Oxford was changing after the war. In spite of the fact that Oxford had chosen to emphasize the humanities, remarkable Oxford scientists had made such discoveries as penicillin (by Fleming) and radar (by Sir Robinson-Watts), and Lord Cherwell was later to become Churchill's scientific advisor. This led to the expansion of a new suburb of central Oxford, The Parks. Churchill realized that we had entered a new war, a war of science and technology. New colleges were needed for young scientists. St. Catherine's, which had been a hall of residence for students, was refounded as St. Catherine's College by Alan

Bullock, a historian who researched the life and death of Hitler. He appointed me a lecturer of the college, about the same time as Tolkien's son. The new college buildings were founded on the flood plain of the river Cherwell, near its confluence with the Thames. Appropriately for such fenland, a Danish architect was selected. The ceremony for laying the foundation stone, performed by the Duke of Edinburgh, was held on a rainy day. Standing immediately behind the architect, the Duke joked, "I hope the whole thing doesn't sink!" The architect, misunderstanding the quick remark, responded, "Yes, your majesty, I hope it does."

Chapter Seven

EXTENDING VISION THROUGH A MYSTICAL ENCOUNTER AND LATIN AMERICAN STUDIES

A Mystical Encounter

*D*uring a sabbatical from Oxford in 1961–62, I was invited by the head of the department of geography at the University of Winnipeg—Tom Weir—to temporarily take charge of his department. This is unusual. Normally when you are a visiting professor, you have no administrative responsibilities. Tom was apparently nervous about delegating his office to his local colleagues during his absence, perhaps fearing a revolt while he was away. He knew me through InterVarsity Fellowship circles as a fellow evangelical, and I was to hold the seat for him until he came back.

As a family, we had never thought we would ever visit North America, let alone the cold winters of Winnipeg! Just as we would have done at Oxford, we entertained colleagues and students while we were there. I especially remember two junior colleagues, one of whom had leanings towards fascism, while the other was a socialist. We invited them to learn about Christianity. Before we left, the young socialist had committed his life to the Lord.

That December, I took ten busloads of InterVarsity students from the various universities in Winnipeg to InterVarsity's wonderful Urbana conference. We came back very moved and challenged in our hearts and our faith by what we heard there, particularly by the missionary appeal. Two nights after I arrived back in Winnipeg, I was awakened in the middle of the night to see an intense light at the foot of my bed. Oddly, I didn't feel surprised or even curious, simply deeply convinced I was in the presence of God. I had the same reaction as Saul of Tarsus when he saw a bright light: "Lord, what do you want me to do?"

There was no answer yet. For seven years I waited, until I knew what it was that I had to do: to give up our safe and happy life at Oxford and return to Canada.

When we left Winnipeg in May 1962, we bought a large car to travel with our children through some of the celebrated sights of western North America: Yellowstone National Park, the Grand Canyon, the beaches of Southern California, the Redwoods, and finally back up to Canada—to Victoria, on Vancouver Island. There, I taught summer school for six weeks. Meanwhile, through the recommendation of my friend F. F. Bruce, I was asked to preach six Sundays at Granville Chapel in mainland Vancouver. On the ferry crossings from Vancouver Island, I read Soren Kierkegaard for the first time. He opened my mind to new depths of Christian understanding. I still remember sitting on the ferry sundeck, feeling the joy of being a Christian with Kierkegaard as my mentor.

At Granville Chapel, I connected deeply with Marshall Sheppard, an elder there (later, my son Christopher would marry his niece). Marshall had a shoe business, having migrated from pioneer farming in the prairies as a youth. In turn, he wanted to create a place where young people could study the Scriptures. He himself had often ploughed with his Bible on the prongs of his plough, trying to understand it, and to meditate. In continued correspondence with him, the vision of Regent College gradually unfolded. There had been a Bible college in the east side of Vancouver that went defunct in 1962; this created the need for another Bible college.

After fulfilling my preaching commitment at Granville Chapel, my family and I crossed the continent by rail and sailed from Montreal back to England. We were welcomed at Southampton Docks by our extended family—and a new car, which we had exchanged for the car we left in Victoria, and we returned to Oxford.

Expanding Oxford Horizons: Invitation to Latin America

Scots engineers had expanded the influence of its Industrial Revolution into the Americas, building continental railways and creating communities of Scots in cities such as Buenos Aires and Santiago. But politically, in the 1950s we were very ignorant of what was happening with the initiation of land reform and of peasant revolts. Brazil and Argentina had nearly joined the Nazis in the war, prevented only by the adroit creation of the Organization of American States.

In 1965, the US-based Ford Foundation offered funds to create several "Institutes of Latin American Studies" to provide intelligence among major universities in the USA and in Britain, particularly to find out what was happening amid the political turmoil and land reform in that area. (One result of the land reforms in Cuba was the rise of Fidel Castro, largely because of land reform in the vast areas of sugar plantations.) Five of these Institutes would be established in Britain, and Oxford was selected as one of the five. A colleague of mine, Raymond Carr (Professor of Spanish History at New College, next door to Hertford), elected me a lecturer at the new St. Anthony's College for these and other regional studies, and its vice-chairman of Latin American Studies. St. Anthony's College had recently been founded upon the money of multimillionaire Antonin Besse, an Arab arms trader from Aden. I was invited in 1966 to visit the new Institutes at Columbia University and the University of Austin, Texas, and to do that, I was offered a six-month sabbatical from Oxford.

But at Hertford College, where I now was a fellow, crisis was brewing.

Hertford College Crisis, 1967: A Major Crisis of My Life

In 1965, we had appointed a new principal, Lord Robert Hall, who had been Economic Advisor to the British government. We felt privileged to have him; it was a new thing for small colleges to be granted endowments by richer colleges, and Merton College had agreed to grant Hertford a piece of land that had never changed ownership since the fourteenth century. This would enable us to build a third quadrangle in the heart of Oxford. Lord Robert Hall would lead the college and raise additional funds for the building project. Since he'd been involved with big business corporations, we thought he would be a wonderful guy to raise funds for our college.

But at our last board meeting of the academic year, June 1967, he quietly requested that we accept his resignation, as he was getting divorced. He wanted to keep it rather quiet, as he had had "affairs." We had suspected that he had been unfaithful to his wife—but she had been his student, and she clung to him, as long as she could. When she gave up, he didn't want messy publicity. He was not really interested in anything that Hertford could give him; it had always been about the dignity he could give Hertford.

We were stunned by his request. After his withdrawal from the room, my colleagues spoke one after the other: "History will never forgive us if we let this key leader resign!" "After all, these days private morals differ from public morals, and publicly, he is highly esteemed!" Etcetera. All twenty-four of my colleagues voted to persuade him to stay on.

Up to this point in my working life, I had been an almost silent, shy junior member, but on that day at last I broke the spell of my low self-esteem. I spoke up. "As a men's college, why do we require girls to leave at 10 p.m.? Are we deliberately permitting a double standard in the college, one for the students and another for the Senior Common Room? If so, I will resign my fellowship!" I was told I was being too scrupulous: "Houston, you are being histrionic!"

Mercifully, I had already negotiated a leave of absence to teach in the United States. I spent a month at Columbia University in New York, and then I stayed at the University of Texas, Austin, until the end of the year. Both wanted me to stay on. But I hated New York; it was so alienating, and as I looked down from Morningside Heights into Harlem, I felt terribly lonely. In fact, I told my wife that my loneliness had churned up my childhood fear of being alone. Still, I loved the friendliness of Austin, and the way they were seriously investing effort in their Institute of Latin American Studies. They wanted me to be their first director. Frankly, I would have loved to stay—but there was a whisper in my heart, and I was dreaming of other things. The especially significant dream was "What about having a college in Vancouver?" I refused both invitations and returned home for Christmas, thinking that I had no position now at Hertford College.

As I was crossing the Quad in early January, a colleague accosted me, cheerfully congratulating me: I had been appointed the new bursar of Hertford! I would take on the role of negotiating with Merton and the financial responsibilities, with the Economic Fellow being the Investment Bursar. Stunned, I began to think the Lord was giving me a rare experience that would equip me for the future needs of the Bible college in Vancouver.

As Bursar, I now had the benefit of having luncheons privately in my office. My wife and I arranged to meet with the ex-wife of our former principal, Lady Margaret Hall, each Monday for lunch. She was head of the government's developmental council for improving trade in Britain, so she was an economist of note. Yet she was still devastated by the failure of her marriage with Lord Robert Hall, and Rita and I took the opportunity to share our faith with her. After a few meetings, we asked if she would be willing to read John's Gospel with us. The first session, I remember her response as a non-Christian: she could not understand one word of the first chapter! Still, she persisted. The college chaplain, Michael Chantry (a lovely Christian) also helped her, and with the gentle leading of us all, eventually she accepted Christ. Sadly, she later became involved in another marriage that proved disastrous, dying of a broken heart.

I had another colleague, John Bradford, who shared my interest in air photographic interpretation. John had in fact gone to war as an air photographic intelligence officer. After returning, he became an archaeologist, examining air photographs of archaeological sites throughout Italy. In mapping the landscapes, he spotted numerous Etruscan tombs that could be identified as bumps in the photographs. He therefore was directing some remarkable archaeological research. But at the height of his career, he became an alcoholic. The university demanded that he commit himself to an alcoholism center for treatment; otherwise, he would be fired. When the day arrived, and there was no evidence that he had signed the document, my anatomist friend Joe Weiner and I conspired to get him help. He was very canny, and we knew that if we knocked at his door together (as we usually came to him), he wouldn't let us in. So Joe told me to phone from the college and he would knock at the door. The trick worked: since I was on the telephone, John opened the door a crack, and Joe thrust his leg through. He held it open as I rushed over with the document for John to sign. With trembling hands he signed the document, but to no avail. Soon afterward, he too died.

Meanwhile, I kept in touch with Lord Robert Hall, who invited me to the House of Lords dining room for a meal together. Free at last from timidity, I asked him, "I understand you were brought up in an evangelical home in Melbourne?"

"Yes," he responded sadly, "I was, but it means nothing to me!"

The words still ring solemnly in my heart. We can be so near, yet so far, from the gospel of Christ.

Link Between Oxford and Hong Kong

One of my students at Hertford, who succeeded to my fellowship there, was John Patten. His real interest was not geography but politics. He used his position to be elected member of Parliament for the city of Oxford, a position he held from 1979 to 1983. He later became the leader of the movement within Parliament to give Hong Kong its independence in 1997. Another Oxford man was Chris Patten—no relation to John—who was appointed the last governor-general of Hong Kong to execute this policy. He has now been chancellor of Oxford University for many years.

It is perhaps not coincidental in kingdom affairs that the greatest numbers of overseas students attending Regent College have come from Hong Kong, which I have visited many times. On a recent visit there, I was approached by a gentleman after a church service. "Do you recognize me?" he asked. I had to acknowledge I did not. He introduced himself as David Sun and showed me correspondence I had had with him in 1973, when he had wanted to come to Regent. He was then in the Auditor General's office, and I had written, "Do not come to Regent and break off from your job in the Auditor's Department in Hong Kong, but instead take the summer course in Oxford on Public

Administration. This would be far more strategic. Don't resign your position to come to Vancouver." He took my advice. He has been director of audit in Hong Kong, in the office of the audit commissioner, for some years. He is now able to advise another governmental auditor in a national crisis in another country. We both learned from this experience that kingdom business is of much greater importance than institutional self-interests.

Dr. Carl F. H. Henry spent a sabbatical from Trinity Evangelical Divinity College (Deerfield, Illinois) in Oxford, in 1969. Charmed by Oxford, he was astonished I was leaving for the unknown in America. He kindly invited me to be a plenary speaker at a conference on prophecy that he was organizing in Jerusalem. I spoke on "the mark of the Beast" in Revelation 17 as referring to the future threat of technocracy, which was wholly outside of the mind-set of those present; "the fulfillment of prophecy" was sweet music (politically) to the president of Israel, David Ben-Gurion, who was present and supporting the event. There I met Jim Hiskey, who invited me to Washington, DC in 1973. We planned to initiate a summer school at the University of Maryland, and this too became part of my North American future.

Chapter Eight

ADVENTURES WITH MALCOLM MUGGERIDGE AND EXPANDING LATIN AMERICAN HORIZONS

Adventures with Malcolm Muggeridge

*D*uring my time at Hertford College in the mid-1960s, I also served on the board of Mueller's Homes, a faith-based orphanage mission, along with Melvin Capper, a surgeon at Bristol University. We became close friends as we planned how we might encourage young men in the faith. With Dr. Hanton (a physician in Cambridge) and a few others, we started the Young Men's Bible Study Fellowship, which would hold a week's course in an Oxford college each year. Our speakers included F. F. Bruce, Professor of New Testament Studies at Manchester University, and distinguished scientists such as Sir Robert Boyle, head of Britain's space program. One of our early recruits was Leonard Muggeridge, who had been an officer on the western front in Austria, then on leave for a summer break. Leonard had become a conscientious objector when he became a Christian at the first Young Men's Bible Study Conference, at Oxford. He could readily have been court-marshaled by the military, but his father's influence commuted his sentence to several years of charitable community work. He chose to become a baker at St. Albans, feeding the poor. He became a Plymouth brother and elder of the local chapel.

Meanwhile, his father—Malcolm Muggeridge (1903–1990)—had become by popular acclaim of the students of Edinburgh University their Rector. Now this was during the sexual revolution, and they expected him to be as sexually dissolute as they were. His early loose living was infamous, but Muggeridge had become as nauseated with the lifestyle as any alcoholic is with drink. He soon resigned. With young Leonard's encouragement, the chaplain of Hertford (Michael Chantry) and I invited him to preach at Hertford Chapel. We restricted attendance to the college community, but afterwards we assembled a public meeting for the curious student crowds. Gnomelike, perched on the floor of the high table, he faced the derision of the crowd. A tall, long-haired youth in a black cloak stood and asked, "Why was Jesus a man and not a woman?"

The quick response was, "What sex are you?" which ended the evening!

Embracing him later, I said, "After all the derision you have given to Christianity, you can expect to get a lot back!"

Meanwhile, he had written *Jesus Rediscovered*. Friends of ours invited him to a summer cottage on Salt Spring Island, off the coast of Vancouver, in January 1971. Rita and I visited him on several weekends, bringing library books from Regent College to keep him, as he said, "on the straight and narrow," while he wrote his next book, *Jesus, the Man Who Lives*. Then he wrote his autobiography, perhaps the best of the twentieth century: *Chronicles of Wasted Time*. But as editor of *Punch*, he began to go too far, lampooning even the royal family. He was exiled to America for the year of 1973.

Planning for the Lausanne Conference in 1974, as a follow-up to the Jerusalem Conference on Prophecy, Billy Graham and John Stott wanted to focus on evangelism and social responsibility. I was asked what I would think of inviting Henry Kissinger as a plenary lay speaker. Astonished, I reacted that as far as I could see, he didn't have a religious bone in his body! I was asked whom I might suggest, and I recommended Malcolm Muggeridge as both "a celebrity and a Christian." After some persuasion, we traveled together—and in Lausanne Malcolm was installed in the Beau Sejour luxury hotel on the shore of Lake Geneva, and I in my cheap pension up the hill.

Feeling an uncomfortable stranger to evangelical life, he asked me to join him for breakfast the next morning at a small table for two. Immediately, a man strolled up, dressed in an immaculate light blue suit.

"Mr. Muggeridge, we Americans don't wait for an introduction. We introduce ourselves. I am Robert Schuller!"

Malcolm had never heard of him, so he remained silent. Schuller continued.

"Mr. Muggeridge, you will be busy at the conference, so let me make an immediate proposition: We will give you $50,000 to conduct a five-day series of television interviews at the Crystal Cathedral in California."

Abruptly, Malcolm replied, "I'm not interested."

"Well, Mr. Muggeridge, money is no object. We shall offer $100,000."

Malcolm had been reading the passage in Dostoyevsky's *Brothers Karamazov* on the Grand Inquisitor, and he blurted out, "Go away, you nasty man!" As he left, Malcolm said, "Jim, I shouldn't have come!" Uneasily, we went to the hotel lobby to meet Billy Graham, who asked if he'd had a comfortable night. "Very well, thank you, but I doubt whether Jesus would have done."

Spending time walking together, away from the conference, I discovered that a brilliant writer like Muggeridge polishes a new thought like the facets of a diamond. All that week, he and I discussed Malcolm's observation that our new "high rises" have no gargoyles because we take our achievements with such deadly seriousness. He also recited a favorite quote from the poet William Blake:

> This life's dim windows of the soul
> Distorts the heavens from pole to pole
> And leads you to believe a lie
> When you see with, not through, the eye.

Francis Schaeffer also let it be known he wanted to have lunch with Muggeridge.

"Why?" Malcolm asked.

"Well," I suggested, "I suppose he wants to know how soundly you have been converted."

Schaeffer, as was his wont, talked all through the meal, and after we said goodbye, Malcolm's response was, "He didn't give me a chance, did he?"

The address Malcolm gave at Lausanne was entitled: "Living through the Apocalypse," which felt quite out of tune at its time, for it was prophetic. The 1974 Lausanne Covenant, produced a solemn list of fifteen statements establishing "a new age for evangelicals." But Muggeridge, as a new Christian, was very simple in his vocabulary and message. He observed, "Through the window I look out on reality; within, there is only fantasy. Oh the glory of reality, the horror of fantasy! The one, Heaven, the other, Hell—two states as clearly differentiated as are light and darkness, joy and wretchedness, life and death." Then he quoted his friend and favorite philosopher Simone Weil: "Nothing is so beautiful and wonderful, nothing is so full of sweet and perpetual ecstasy, as is the good; no desert is so monotonous and boring as evil. But with fantasy it is the other way around. Fictional good is boring and flat, while fictional evil is varied and intriguing, attractive, profound, and full of charm."

Christianity Today (August 16, 1974) carried a full report on the Lausanne Conference, but with no response whatever to

Muggeridge's plenary address! Presumably, they did not know what to make of his "apocalyptic" message when the rest of the conference was so full of the evangelical movement's cheerful future.

Until now, it had been a toss-up whether he should become a Plymouth brother or a Roman Catholic, for his son Leonard was proving a saint, and so was Mother Teresa, whom he had filmed for the BBC in her Calcutta ministry. Since I would shortly be leaving for six months in Vancouver, I requested that John Stott give Malcolm some pastoral attention. But he did not, so on my return to London, I asked, had he seen Malcolm? He hadn't, so together we travelled by train from Charing Cross to Robertsbridge, Malcolm's home near Brighton. At the station, awaiting the same train, was the Irish Lord, Frank Packenham, leader of the Catholic lobby in the House of Lords. His estate was near Robertsbridge.

"Now, you chaps," he said to us, as we sat in the compartment, "why has Malcolm become a Catholic?"

We all laughed, because Lord Longford had brought Malcolm and Kitty into the Catholic Church. Also, on his estate Longford had provided a home for "mentally retarded" children, who attended his private chapel. Malcolm also loved the mentally handicapped children. We agreed it was the care of the mentally handicapped that was Muggeridge's simple ecclesiology, nothing else!

Malcolm Muggeridge died in 1990 and Lord Longford in 2001, both having ended living simple, beatific lives with their spouses. I have never been more inspired by humility than I have been by theirs. Indeed, Longford published a booklet on *Humility*, and Kitty Muggeridge wrote on the *Heavenly Gaze*.

Expanding Latin American Horizons: Vice-Chairman of Latin American Studies, Oxford

In the latter part of 1969, I was sent to eighteen Latin American countries, to negotiate academic relations. I began in Guatemala, Honduras, El Salvador, Costa Rica, and then went to all the countries of southern America except Bolivia. Memorable was the visit to Colombia, where an American economist had created a first-class university in Bogota, the University of the Andes.

Visits to missionaries were on my private agenda, so I visited a widow—Catherine Morgan—in Pasto, Colombia, on its Andean border with Ecuador. She and her husband had effectively nursed many sick people in their old house. Maliciously, ground glass was put into the food of her husband and he had been killed. Regardless of her loss, she soldiered on in her ministry as a nurse, impressing me greatly by her courage and dedication. Yet she was surprised that I would ever go out of my way to visit her. Her old colonial home was overflowing from every room into the corridors with the beds of the sick. I continued to receive letters from her, telling me on one occasion that she had taken a canoe trip down one of the Amazon headwaters, to spend the night in a native settlement. Two brothers in a drunken quarrel led to the death of one; quite happily, she slept that night between a corpse and his killer. It was all part of her routine! (That same day, in the post with her letter, was another from an orphanage in Italy, where the "missionary" had absconded with the funds—a contrast between light and darkness!) Later, Catherine Morgan became the mentor of Elisabeth Elliot, one of the widows whose husbands had been killed by a small band of Auca Indians. Her story is well told in *Through Gates of Splendor*. Jim Elliot, her husband, was uncle to two of my sons-in-law—a wonderful heritage!

My southern destination was Buenos Aires, to link with the Institute of Economics. I had three cousins there, so I arranged that the middle brother's five-year-old son, Alejandro, would eventually exchange with our middle daughter, Claire—he to learn English in Oxford, and she to learn Spanish in Buenos Aires—before each of them entered junior school (the end of that story will be told later). I then returned to Mexico City, as the guest of the British Council, and to be with Rita at the end of a long absence.

After my tour, I began sending doctoral students to troubled spots—like El Salvador, before its civil war, and to the Santa Marta Mountains of northern Colombia, later the headquarters of the Farc insurgents. I was still supervising their work when we started Regent College. Like the insurgents in the Philippines today, most of them are ethnically different, merely restless with the corruption of the central government. It is the international press, ill-informed of the local context, who highlight their struggles. Of course, there are criminal gangs as well.

Chapter Nine

THE TRAGEDY
OF OUR LITTLE JONATHAN

As the bursar of Hertford College, I actually found it easy to fundraise for the new quadrangle. We had the connections, and our aim was strategic for the expansion of Oxford education. By contrast, our experience with beginning to fundraise for Regent College was exactly the opposite: not at all easy, lacking the credibility of a centuries-old university connection, and not wanting to ask friends for money. A friend is an unconditional friend, and I never would ask one of them for money. We did, however, hold two summer schools in Vancouver as a tryout exercise.

Unexpectedly, Rita became pregnant in 1967, the year we decided to go to Vancouver. I was already teaching our first summer school there, and I knew I would be late for the birth. During the week of summer school, I was told, "You have a son." Apparently, all was well.

With great joy, I stepped out of the London airport and was greeted by Nesta, my sister-in-law, to rush to the hospital and see my newborn little boy. We were already calling him Jonathan. But Nesta looked very sad. I thought, *What's wrong?* She only told me, "We are not going direct to Oxford."

Once out of the suburbs, she stopped in a cornfield to inform me, "You have a Down Syndrome child. Tomorrow morning, you will have to decide whether to operate to remove a stomach blockage, or allow the child to die." Immediately, the golden sunshine was turned to metallic brass.

That evening, I knelt on the couch groaning, "God, how can you call us to Regent but now make it impossible? The immigration authorities will refuse our entry into Canada with a Down Syndrome baby. And what if Rita and I do not agree on what to do?"

It came to me like a voice from heaven, "You have no prerogative to take life. You have to accept life, not destroy it." Yet I knew this might forfeit our call to emigrate to Vancouver. I prayed that when I returned to the hospital the next morning, Rita and I would be of one mind in the decision.

The next morning, in fear and trembling, I went to Rita's bedside. Very brightly she responded, "Of course we operate, don't we?" The gynecologists operated, but they failed to remove the obstruction, and complications ensued. Within a week, Jonathan died. I did not know at the time that my wife's words, coming dazed out of the anaesthesia, had been to mutter to the surgeon, "I wish it had never been born."

At a women's retreat in Zurich twenty-five years later, she confessed the guilt that she felt to a small group of ladies. Sobbing, she added, "I wonder if the surgeon heeded my reactionary cry and botched the operation. If so, I killed my child!"

A Welsh lady, Mary Lewis from Cardiff, was present. Her husband, Tony Lewis, had been a gynecologist/obstetrician in the Oxford hospital at the time. Immediately she phoned Tony, asking if he remembered the event. "Yes," he said, "I remember it vividly, because I was the surgeon on duty who delivered that child. We tried all we could, to save him in the operation. We did everything possible to save that child's life."

After twenty-five years of secret guilt, Rita realized that all was well. The trauma of losing little Jonathan affected our whole family, bringing us all much closer together. We began to tell our story when we arrived in Vancouver, especially to others who had Down Syndrome children, some of whom named their sons Jonathan. Rita's older sister, Nesta (who had met me at the London airport), already had a mentally handicapped daughter, Sheila. Sheila is now sixty, the soul of the village where she lives. Everybody knows that she loves Jesus, and she is a lovely witness of God's love.

When Jonathan was born, Rita told Christopher, but not the younger girls. When Jonathan died, Claire said she had intuitively known there was a serious handicap with her little brother. This profoundly affected her, for Claire remembered his birth on August 17 and his death, August 21, ever afterward. She wanted to have a son that she would call Jonathan, which she joyously did have years later! Other friends facing the same trial have since named their son Jonathan.

How were our other children affected? Very differently. Christopher lost the opportunity to have a brother. He grieved silently on his own. Penny was relieved that she was still spoilt as the youngest, asking her mum to work through such "wicked feelings," which Rita fully understood herself. Yet she also remembers being at our bedside to pray together, and to share grief. What deeply affected her was the mentally handicapped cousin, Sheila, which motivated Penny later to volunteer to work at the Mueller Orphanage in Bristol. Lydele was away at a holiday camp at Bude, and never knew he was sick, so it came as a great shock to her when he died so quickly. Claire, as I have indicated, was heartbroken, so that our German au pair, Ursula, took her alone to Bude, for a short holiday, so that her mother could rest.

In June 1970, we were given a year's leave of absence without pay from Hertford, and we emigrated as a family to Vancouver, with no immigration obstructions.

Chapter Ten

THE FOUNDING
OF REGENT COLLEGE

*W*e had planned in late 1967 that we would begin our
new Bible college with two summer schools in 1968
and 1969. I had been involved in creating an Oxford summer
school for young men for some fourteen years, so I was aware
of their fruitfulness. If these two summer schools succeeded in
gaining numbers, we would start a one-year Diploma of Christian
Studies, and if we could receive affiliation with the University of
British Columbia (UBC) there in Vancouver, we would eventually
offer a Master of Christian Studies degree. We were further
gratified that Harvard Theological School also began a Master of
Christian Studies program, so we would not be the only college
offering such an unusual new degree.

Remarkable coincidences encouraged us beyond our
wildest dreams. We did not realize that only western Canada had
legislation that allowed universities to appoint affiliate colleges
with independent governance. As the agricultural frontier had
moved west, each stage had established an agricultural college
for the colonists, as affiliates of McGill University. As these
agricultural colleges became universities in each provincial

capital, they in turn provided for affiliates, either as halls of residence for students, or as seminaries. Later, we discovered this was unique in all the world of academia.

At Oxford, in the summer of 1968, I invited F. Kenneth Hare (1919–2002), professor of climatology at London University, to dine with me in college. He had told me he was leaving to take up a post as vice-chancellor of the University of British Columbia. Surprised, I told him that I too hoped to go to Vancouver, and I told him our plans. "Over the cups," he responded. "Well, you will need library privileges," which he promised would be arranged.

Then I discovered that his wife was a devout Christian, and he briefly supported our cause. But during student revolts, he suffered a nervous breakdown. He retired to be appointed the University of Toronto's first government scientific advisor on environmental affairs, in 1970. I also learned that the dean of academic planning at UBC was a devout Christian, and strongly supported our application for affiliation.

Meanwhile, two young friends at Granville Chapel, Ken Smith and Don Bennett, promised to find a home for our family. Ken also suggested we use the name of his business, Regent Development Company, for our college name, since something needed to be registered at the government office in Victoria. We had sought in vain for a Christian saint's name that would be distinct. Later, a hymn writer volunteered to compose a hymn for our graduation—and without knowing the origin of the college's name, called upon "Regents of our God and King" to praise him!

Major-General Sir Ouvry Roberts (1898–1986) had been sent to Vancouver in retirement, as the Duke of Westminster's land agent, to buy West Vancouver property for a dollar per acre. In return, the Duke would build Lions' Gate Bridge, to replace the old ferry. Now widowed, he had remarried a young wife who did not want to be left stranded in the wilderness of British Columbia. She urged him to sell their house and return to England, where their two boys were in boarding school. The market was dead, and they had found no takers on their house for over a year. My friends thought the house would suit our family well, having a bedroom for each child as well as a guest room. It was near schools and close to Granville Chapel. He had also lowered the price, so that it became affordable for us. Further, we discovered that if we exchanged properties instead of both selling our homes, we would not be taxed and lose 25 percent of our savings, as would have happened if we sold our houses and brought the funds to Canada. So, sight unseen by both parties, we exchanged homes. Sir Ouvry then flew over to visit us. As meticulous as you might expect a former controller general to be, he listed all he would leave behind—from his old Humber car in the garage to the lavatory brush in the bathroom. These basic furnishings served us for the first weeks in our Vancouver home, until our container sailed into port with our family furnishings.

As a devout Anglican, Sir Ouvry was impressed by our vision for Regent College. A luncheon was organized by his small select club of leaders of British Columbia, but rather than give his own speech, he asked me to address them. Present were the two archbishops, Anglican and Catholic, the three university vice chancellors, and the former federal minister of justice, Davie Fulton. Immediately, the Anglican archbishop promised to see if the Presbyterian college on the campus would house our students in their basement. Davie Fulton, representing the law faculty in the senate and the CEO of Cominco mining company, stood in our favor for affiliation—as did the alumni representative on the senate.

Our children marveled at all this, saying "God really wants us here, doesn't he!"

Across the road from us, the dean of the Anglican Cathedral, Herbert O'Driscoll, had each of our senior faculty preach on aspects of their research in an evening series the next year. Later, local medical specialists agreed to give a series of public lectures on Christian perspectives in their fields of study. Regent was beginning to be respected by a broadening community.

I was sent on a fundraising assignment for Regent College in October 1970, to approach John Templeton (1912–2008), who was then living in Nassau. A humble and modest man, Sir John was called by *Money Magazine* in 1999 "the greatest global stock picker of the century." He gave away over a billion dollars, which in those days was a lot more. He had been a faithful, loyal trustee of Princeton Seminary for forty-two years, having already given them about 125 million dollars when I met with him. But my trip proved a dead end. At that time, he was fixed on one charitable pursuit: to establish a Nobel Prize in religion. The Nobel trustees turned him down. Instead, in 1972 he created the Templeton Foundation, to award scholars uniting science and faith. Anyway, I returned empty-handed from Nassau.

But unexpectedly, a Chinese immigrant to Vancouver, businessman David Lam, invited me out for lunch and asked—as a joke, I thought—"Jim, what would you do if somebody offered you a million dollars for Regent College?"

I replied, "I have often dreamed that someone, someday might actually do so. I have had plenty of time to think of my response."

With a laugh, he asked, "What is your response?"

"Oh, I have prayed about it, but I don't think we are morally ready for so much money as a million dollars."

He looked at me with obvious surprise and said, "Perhaps then, I can give the college their first million to build a chapel"— and so Regent College's chapel is named after him.

We later had an alumnus, Rob Alloway, who spent a lot of time with me in personal counseling. Rob came from a wealthy family in Toronto, and his father was in the printing industry. His donations established Regent's bookstore as a commercial operation, and his sister Heather later gave Regent the money to build the tower that is now such a landmark on the campus.

We started emphasizing "marketplace theology" in 1970, and it has been a Regent College buzzword ever since. We also envisaged attracting and sending our students worldwide, so we have maintained an affiliation with the InterVarsity movement. We began to invite distinguished scientists to teach at our summer schools, so we could begin to speak knowledgeably about science and faith. One of the first was Walter Thorson, trained at Caltech, and professor of theoretical chemistry at the University of Alberta in Edmonton.

We began to issue a quarterly College Bulletin in the spring of 1971. Our first issue was on "The Importance of Being on a University Campus." From the start, we wanted to promote the genuine relationship between the Christian faith and true scholarship. I had been to the University of Chicago as a guest of a friend, visiting their faculty club. On its walls were the university shields of the Ivy League universities; many had Christian mottoes, such as Princeton ("Under God's guidance it flourishes"), Columbia ("In thy Light we see light"), etc. Inspired, I realized that we needed to be a renewed light at UBC—for the mottoes were no longer true nor relevant at many universities. When asked what guarantee we could give for the future of Regent College, soberly we admitted we could not make such a pledge; we could only pray that Regent would continue to be "Christian" and never secularized by "Christian scholarship."

In the autumn of 1971, I spelled out in our Bulletin "the Christian way of knowing," emphasizing seven vital attitudes.

1. The love of God is the primary requisite for the love of Truth. For without faith in God, any system for understanding is inadequate.

2. No knowledge is more important than biblical knowledge, so that the study of the Scriptures requires scholarly exegesis as the basis of wisdom and grappling with contemporary problems.

3. Christian philosophy cannot be a substitute for the simple attention to God's word. (There had been a twin Institute

established in Toronto by some Dutch Reformed scholars, and on a visit, they asked me how were we different from them. "Oh," I said, "if you have ten faculty members you will have nine philosophers and one theologian—but we will have nine theologians and one philosopher.")

4. All meaningful conceptions gained in biblical study must be related to personal and social life. It is the formation of Christian character and conduct that is essential, not just being an academic factory that manufactures products called "degrees" and "diplomas."

5. "Let the Word of God dwell in you richly," for nothing is more vital than the personal nature of a living faith. Personal/ pastoral concern for our staff and board members, and each individual student, must have the highest priority.

6. The Christian life is valueless without personal sacrifice. We still encourage our students to realize that one of their most significant experiences at Regent is having taken time out from their careers, including the sacrifice of time and money required to attend the courses.

7. Finally, "to know" is also "to witness." We expect our students and staff to lead others to Christ, not from a rigid duty of talking about the truth (like some other arising student movements), but from the joyous spontaneity of knowing God's word and responding to it.

"Pray for us, that we may be kept faithful to the task of the gospel," was our final sentence.

I began the second year's Bulletin by quoting Victor Hugo's remark that "nothing is so powerful as the idea whose time has come." The very idea behind Regent College is that "the doctrine of the priesthood of all believers" is not just something to practice in the church building, but it is a call for every Christian to use all his or her gifts and training primarily to serve God, and only secondarily for his/her own advancement in a secular career. As a missionary to India, William Carey had said: "I make shoes to earn my bread and butter, but my business is to serve God." It had started in the early church: Peter was a fisherman, Matthew was a civil servant, and Paul was a tentmaker, but the primary task of each was to be a messenger of God. Some of our church leaders did not like this message, assuming it was an echo from the Plymouth Brethren! But with this message I made four points:

1. As life gets more complex, more narrowly defined skills develop which require more cross-disciplinary cooperation. The newly arising great ethical issues of our day, in biology, medicine, business, education, and politics, require responsible Christians to integrate biblical scholarship with scientific knowledge.

2. In an age of dissolving authority, fashion reigns. But fashion is a not a good ruler, because it is governed not by rules but by whim and fancy. Christians need the insights of biblical wisdom and the strength of Christian convictions, to resist the fashionable as a substitute for the authoritative.

3. The role of science and the nature of knowledge need critical reappraisal today. (I was being influenced by the thought of Michael Polanyi, whom I mentioned earlier.)

4. As leisure increases and life is prolonged, retirement comes earlier, and the mobility of professional careers has intensified the opportunity for Christian training to be increased in later life. This needs to be imaginative, flexible, and continuous.

These Bulletins flowed into the 1980s, by which time *Crux* magazine, started by the Toronto Graduate Christian Fellowship, was passed on to Regent as our quarterly journal.

During our first five years, we held classes in the basement of the Vancouver School of Theology. Then, perhaps because of our growing number of students, we were asked to find another location. A Baptist developer had bought some of the only freehold land on the UBC campus—the rest of the campus land all being leasehold, in order to thwart the municipality from building a high-rise. On this land, at the edge of UBC, stood two of the three freehold-land fraternity houses on campus. At a rate reduced from what he had paid for them, $500,000, he offered the property to us. We managed to borrow the money. Stan Cummings, the father-in-law of our early supporter Don Bennett—a retired postal official and handyman—began to renovate the fraternity property and turn it into our college. Our families all lent a hand, scrubbing the blackened windows of the initiation room while Stan transformed the kitchen and dining room in our lecture hall. He had to redo all the electrical wiring and plumbing.

Meanwhile, in 1974, Phil Hill was appointed professor of mechanical engineering at UBC. A brilliant inventor, he later pioneered a process for transforming a diesel engine to use natural gas. His wife Margaret volunteered to be our first librarian and bookstore manager, in rented huts on the site. Much later, her daughter Tricia similarly volunteered to operate InterVarsity's first Center for Christian Study at the University of Virginia in Charlottesville.

Funding for Regent was terribly tight at first, so those of us who could also teach at UBC did so. Dr. W. J. (Bill) Martin had been Director of Oriental Studies at the University of Liverpool, so the Religion Department at UBC was glad to employ him. I taught environmental ethics at the university's Geography Department. These connections actually helped Regent College later, in our application for affiliation with the university; our supporters, in vigorous debate in the University Senate, argued "Why turn them down, when these departments want them full time?" Neither Bill nor I was paid by Regent College until 1977. From the start, our faculty, staff, and students have made great financial sacrifices to be at Regent, especially as Vancouver has become an increasingly expensive city to live in.

Students attracted to my environmental ethics course at UBC included young lawyers and political scientists who later created the Greenpeace Movement. Ironically, the parents of the founder of Greenpeace, David McTaggart, were Christians who attended Granville Chapel, but he had rebelled against

Christianity. He did not know I was teaching his UBC associates, and when they invited me to their first year's celebration, he asked me, aghast, "What are you doing here?" He looked horrified, and I believe he felt haunted by his religious past! Greenpeace's idealism later turned sour, due to internal rivalries. It collapsed, a warning to all new institutional movements.

Celebrating the first section of the building of Regent College,
which is still not yet completed.

The fiftieth anniversary of our wedding
with our children and grandchildren on our son's farm in Ontario.

One of my early students at Oxford, Major General John Grinald,
visiting a sick little boy who died shortly after.

My wife and I at the retreat in Washington, DC at the first stage of her
Alzheimer's disease. Amused by her own forgetfulness.

Malcolm Muggeridge, on the visit to Salt Spring Island off the coast of
Vancouver, when his friend was renting the summer cottage for his writing.
I was giving him books from Regent College library
to keep me theologically on the straight and narrow.

Kraus Bockmuehl, a distinguished evangelical scholar
in Germany who was persuaded to come to be the first
professor of systematic theology at Regent College.

Dr. Bill Marton, former director of Oriental studies at Liverpool University, who was appointed as Regent's first professor of the Old Testament study.

The home at Heemstede North of Amsterdam
that belongs to Ernst and Erica van Eeghen.

Ernst and Erica van Eeghen.

The public park in Albacete where my mother nursed us small children.

Sitting beside Don Quixote, on my left, and Sancho Panza.

An original steam engine, no doubt driven by my father's friend who returned his loan to my father when there was no food on our table.

My favorite saint, St. Teressa, deeply influenced my life.

A bast of Fr. Ximenes de Cisneros, the confessor of Isabella la Catolica and primate of the Catholic Church, that was commissioned by her to create the University of Alcala de Henares.

With my two daughters, Penny and Lydele, at Albacete.

Chapter Eleven

OUR FIRST STUDENTS, OUR FIRST YEARS, AT REGENT—AND A FEW DISTINGUISHED ALUMNI

Our First Students, Our First Years

*W*hat then about our first students? Following the precedent we had established at Oxford for fourteen years of having an annual summer school for young men, we held our first Regent summer school in 1968. In 1970, we were ready to accept diploma students. Two Texan Marine veterans, having had their lives saved in Vietnam, were the first to come to the college. Late that summer they were staying in our home, but they decided to attend the wedding of one of their war buddies and return within the week for the start of classes. Their parents urged me to dissuade them from taking such a crazy journey, but they insisted. Traveling with them as far as San Francisco, to be a bridesmaid, was Diane Pinreid, another student—the daughter of the high commissioner of the Salvation Army for western Canada.

On a divided highway at dusk, in Oregon, an old man in a large car ploughed into their small Vauxhall. All three young people were killed.

It was a memorial service I will never forget, as I envisaged their spilled blood on the road. In "O Love That Wilt Not Let Me Go," the beautiful hymn of George Mathieson, he states in the third stanza "and from the ground, there blossoms red, life that shall endless be." I cited that line at the service, firmly believing that God would honor their apparently wasted lives with a special blessing for the future of the college.

Four students graduated with their diplomas at our first convocation: David Karsgaard, who later ranked high in the Canadian Foreign Office; Stan Riegel, a scientist; Massimo Rubboli, later an Italian philosopher professor; and Peter Shaw, later a senior executive of the British Education Ministry and now teaching in our new Institute of Leadership. Our first convocation speaker was Robert Clark, dean of academic planning at UBC. He had strongly supported our application for affiliation, which was granted in 1974. We then could offer the Master of Christian Studies degree.

Just a Few of Our Distinguished Alumni

Several more early Regent alumni were to distinguish themselves later. In 1973, Sandy Sharpe came to us from Washington, DC. She had been a curator/artist for the curator of the National Library, and plainly she had artistic abilities. But she obviously also had diplomatic abilities as well. After her time at our college, she was appointed—despite the interruption of her career—to be an official hostess at Blair House, Washington's private guest house for visiting presidents and other dignitaries. She served all these distinguished persons for a number of years, and since then she has been very much involved in the National Prayer Breakfast movement and the C. S. Lewis Institute. There will be a good deal more about Sandy Sharpe and both those organizations in a later chapter, which will cover our horizons in Washington, DC.

John Innes was another early Regent student. Upon arriving in 1971, he wrote the beautiful and remarkably mature poem, "Re: Dis-covered by my Constant Lover," from which I draw the beautiful line about "Transforming lonely 'I' to glorious 'We.'" John had been adopted at the age of four months, unwanted by a wealthy old Montreal family who disapproved of their daughter marrying a poor husband. She was forced to give John up for adoption by conservative, elderly Christian parents in Toronto. John stayed in Rita's and my home for three years while studying at the college, and after spending Christmas with us in 1971, he always considered Christmas with us a high priority. In spite of his many travels after leaving Regent, he returned to celebrate Christmas with our families in Vancouver almost every year. While I was composing this section, John—now sixty-nine— came to see me after some absence between us, and he told me this remarkable story. Recently, via DNA testing, he discovered a cousin of his seven siblings, and then the siblings themselves. Apparently, his father had muttered something about "Baby John" being given up for adoption when on his deathbed; twenty years later, the informant finally took the information seriously. After sixty-nine years, John was reunited with his original family. All of his siblings have gone into the arts professionally—a younger sister is a well-known Canadian singer—and drama particularly runs throughout the family. John has been a lifelong actor, performing at the Stratford Festival in Ontario, Bard on the Beach in Vancouver, many other American theaters, and more recently, in television films. All this has deepened his faith, and he tells me he has embraced his own poem as never before.

The same year that Sandy Sharpe joined us—1973—I received a request from a shop girl in Penticton in the Okanagan Valley, Janet Martin. She said, "I am too poor to have earned a university degree, but I wonder if I could fulfill my dreams by coming to Regent College to do the one-year diploma without a prior degree." It is still a policy of the University, which we follow, to include a 10 percent discretionary admission for mature students. She entered under the category of "mature student" after writing me an essay on the subject of "Theology as a Metaphor." I thought it was a very bright essay. She did come, and earned her Diploma. She applied to Cornell University, and on the premise of the same essay that she had given me, they gave her a full scholarship to do a doctorate. Then she had it published by Oxford University Press—and after that, she was appointed a lecturer at Oxford. Later, I walked across the cobblestones between colleges with her and said, "Janet, now you are going to be a full professor of theology." My prediction was correct. As Janet Martin Soskice, she was appointed by Cambridge to be a full professor, and then she became the first woman to chair the whole faculty of theology. Janet has written a very amusing and semi-autobiographical story of two ladies in Sinai, and she keeps in touch with us at Regent. She is a delight.

Another distinguished Regent student, a skilled medical doctor in Singapore before he arrived in Vancouver—Dr. Hua-Soo Ming—decided after Regent that he and his little family should go to Szechuan in southwest China. He offered his services to the government of Szechuan to provide medical services throughout the province, setting up clinics in remote towns. The network became so impressive that he was given the award, "The friend of Szechuan"; the next year, the politburo gave him a national award named for Norman Bethune, the medical doctor who walked the Thousand-Mile trek with the communist leaders, and who was named a "Friend of China." Remarkably, Dr. Hua-Soo Ming is now the second such holder of the politburo's award, "The Friend of China." He now works in the Department of Social Studies at the University of Singapore.

A more recent Malaysian student is the senior executive of one of Malaysia's government corporations. He is the first Christian—certainly the first evangelical—to ever head an Islamic public corporation. He is a remarkable witness in Malaysia.

We have had numerous distinguished students from all walks of life, and we have been immensely blessed by too many distinguished alumni to mention. But one more whom I must mention is Edwin Hui. He had been a distinguished doctor; he was elected unanimously by his forty-nine Jewish colleagues to be CEO of the Jewish Hospital in Los Angeles, although he was the only Christian practicing there. Unfortunately, over the course of his career he had neglected his faith. When he was diagnosed with liver cancer, his surgeon had to cut as close to the liver as he could—and saved his life in a spectacular way. Soberly, Dr. Hui realized he should make a renewal of commitment to his Lord after neglecting his faith for so long. In 1989, he came to Regent to do a master's degree, and then—because of his remarkable abilities—we appointed him to hold a joint fellowship of medical ethics at the faculty of medicine at UBC and Regent College. He is the only one to hold a joint appointment between the university and Regent in all the time since we, as founders (myself and Bill Martin) held similar appointments with Regent and UBC at the beginning.

Edwin Hui is now the chairman of our Chinese Studies program. Because of the skills and abilities he has displayed to Chinese universities, Regent is now recognized as the external examiner for the only Doctor in Christian Studies that is allowable in the universities of China. They do have a comparative religion section of university training in China. Ten scholarly magazines are allowed to circulate—the others are, of course, in Buddhist, Taoist, and Confucian studies—but there was no Christian journal until this time. It's what we publish, *Regent Review of Christian Thought*; but most of our faculty has never read it because it is in Chinese! Still, it has been published every year for several decades. We also have the privilege of welcoming Chinese students in comparative religion to Regent from August to December, to help them choose a thesis topic and to be given guidance as to how they might develop it when they go back to China. Here is one wonderful example of what has happened.

Last year, a young Chinese woman came to me and said, "You know, I have always wanted to establish in the Chinese university 'children's studies,' but it doesn't exist. Can you help me select a topic for launching this program in Chinese universities, so that my department can specialize in studies for Chinese children?"

I said, "Have you ever read the Narnia tales by C. S. Lewis?"

She hadn't—and she did. In fact, she was charmed by them. By Christmas, she had become a Christian. She was baptized before she went back to China. Such a wonderful emissary, and how wonderful it is that God has used these different international relationships.

Yet it is invidious to name only distinguished students. For so many have been so sacrificial and the costs have been so high. Just recently, one lady reminded me she had been stalked by a predator while at Regent, and found safety in living with us after the event. Another was raped in Stanley Park. Like the list of the faithful in Hebrews 11, many never enjoyed promising professional futures because they came to Regent instead! As expressed in *Joyous Exiles*, many have deliberately embraced "the Hidden Life."

Chapter Twelve

FURTHER
LATIN AMERICAN HORIZONS

For Lack of a Swiss Pocketknife,
a Medieval Castle is Built

I continued to travel widely during Regent College's early years. On one of my trips to Brazil with my translator, Bob Moon, we visited and addressed churches in Recife, in the northeast. Bob's uncle was a wealthy businessman, in control of sugar production, cement, and brewing industries. He invited Bob and me for Sunday lunch. As we sat in a baronial hall, within a medieval-style castle with some thirty family and guests, he told me his story.

As a small boy, he had longed to own a Swiss pocketknife, but his father was too poor to give him one. So later he began collecting knives, and eventually bought out an old company of Sheffield cutlery, including their museum collection. Still not content, he began to visit antique dealers in Spain, where he collected medieval armor—even that of a knight on his horse, with his spear and chivalric banner! But where to put them all?

He had a medieval castle built outside Recife, to house the collection. Sitting beside me at lunch were his two single daughters. One was the director of his museum, while the other was director of tourism for the museum. All because a small boy had been thwarted from having a Swiss pocketknife!

Ricardo Barbosa, Pastor to Pastors in Brazil

In 1989 (and where he woud remain until 1991), Brazilian pastor Ricardo Barbosa was sent to Regent College, where he hoped to graduate as a church pastor. Failing to master the biblical languages, he did a Master's degree with me in spiritual theology instead. He returned to become nationally recognized as a "pastor to pastors," gaining far more recognition than if he had succeeded in earning a Master of Divinity degree. He has arranged all my visits to Brazil since then. More recently, he has become pastor to Maria da Silva (a candidate for the presidential election in October 2018).

Maria herself has a remarkable story, for as an Amazonian teenager of fifteen, she was abandoned by her parents and adopted by a small community of Catholic nuns, who baptized her, named her Maria da Silva, i.e., "Mary of the forest," and taught her Portuguese. In her mid-twenties, she was elected to run an environmental movement to help save the Amazon, after the previous leader was assassinated by timber barons. She attracted the attention of President "Lula," who appointed her the first federal minister of the environment, but after facing a losing battle against local corruption, she resigned in 2008. Maria da Silva has survived at least four assassination attempts. Meeting with her twice in the last two years, I have connected her with Christian government officials from two other countries, to prepare for a less corrupt governance.

And as I mentioned earlier, one of our recent Regent alumni—as deputy prosecutor of Curitiba—put President "Lula" behind bars after his corruption conviction in 2018.

Dieter Brepthol and Lapinha, the "Spa of the Americas"

I met Dieter Brepthol and his wife Margaret in 1984, at their home at Curitiba in Brazil, when he took me to stay at his spa some twenty-five kilometers south of the city. His Austrian grandmother had emigrated at the turn of the twentieth century to what was then a wilderness, buying an extensive property that included a remnant of primeval forest along a river valley, and hot springs, which she intended to turn into a spa like those she had known in Austria and Switzerland. Three years before my visit, Dieter had inherited this property. But Dieter had been "called" to become president of InterVarsity in Brazil, and later InterVarsity president for all Latin America. He shared with me that he felt a deep tension about this call, and that he had already delegated others to run the spa, but the other management was proving unsuccessful. How could God seem to give him two contradictory "callings?" I urged him to see that God was now giving him a far more strategic mission, to influence the rich and the famous, whereas many others could lead a student movement. He accepted the greater vision and turned out to be a great businessman. Lapinha has been rated since 2013 as the top spa in the Americas, and even one of the world's ten top spas. The whole team of doctors and therapists are Christians. Recently, it has expanded to serve as a dietary spa as well. In the evenings are concerts and lectures on a variety of topics, always with a Christian theme; I have contributed on several visits. The adjoining primeval forest is committed to become part of a national nature reserve.

Rescued from Kidnapping by a Child's Basic Trust

As I stated earlier, we forget that Brazil and Argentina had nearly joined the Nazi Axis during the Second World War. Nazi war criminals remained hidden there until these countries became democracies—in Argentina, as late as four years ago. On my extensive 1969 trip to Latin America as vice-chairman of Latin American studies, my last negotiation had been with the prestigious Institute of Economics in Buenos Aires. I have mentioned that my Uncle Charles was no longer alive, but that I spent a pleasant week with his three sons. The middle son, Edward, had a single child, Alejandro, the same age as our daughter Claire, and we had come to an agreement that Claire would study Spanish in Buenos Aires, while Alejandro came to Oxford to learn English. But the next Spring, there was a clampdown on news from Buenos Aires, and we lost touch.

The oldest cousin's granddaughter, Melina, was searching the internet about seven years ago when she discovered that there was a "Houston" at Regent College, Vancouver, a possible relative. We got in touch, and when I told her the address of the family business firm in Buenos Aires that I had visited in 1968, that confirmed we were from the same "Houston" family. She did not know what had happened to her great-uncle Alejandro, but as he had married a Paraguayan, she had always assumed they had gone there, perhaps to hide. Through Ricardo Barbosa's sister-in-law in Brasilia, I was eventually put in touch with my second cousin, Alejandro. In September 2017, I visited their home in Asuncion, Paraguay. Finally I heard the full story of his kidnapping.

Alejandro was much loved by his parents, and as a child, he was unafraid and venturesome. In a word: trusting. Peeking through the gates of his kindergarten school one day, three men offered him candy. He stepped out to receive it and was snatched into their car—for a joyride, or so he thought—but only when evening fell did he feel concerned that his parents would not know where he was. The next night, when the men were snoring in their sleep, he crept out into the darkest suburbs of northeast Buenos Aires—again unafraid, for he saw a house light in the distance. It was the home of a kindly Catholic family, who welcomed him in. Asked for his father's phone number, he was able to give it immediately, for he frequently phoned home. Upon receiving the call, his parents fled in their nightclothes, snatched him up, and drove directly to Asuncion, where they remained.

Alejandro's thirteen-year-old son is as unafraid as his father. Now a film producer, Alejandro took his boy into the wildest part of South America, the Chaco region of Argentina, to film for a rancher. Then only eight years old, he took out his fishing rod and almost immediately shouted, "Daddy, I've caught a fish … no I haven't, I've caught a crocodile!" Racing to the lake bank, the rancher lassoed a six-foot-plus monster, turned it on its back to extract the fishing hook from its jaws, and let it slide back into the lake.

It's the way a child lives, when there is a heritage of basic trust! This July, we are having a reunion of the Houston clan, from Latin America, Canada, and Scotland, at my son's home.

But since we made contact with our kidnapped relative, we have learned that the kidnapping of untold thousands from 1978 until 2015 created "the Generation of the Disappeared Ones," a South American holocaust. By the hundreds, kidnapped children and young people were herded onto military transport aircraft and pitched into the Atlantic. Only this year, the first fourteen criminal military officers have been tried in the International Court of The Hague. It is a chilling story still to be revealed and told.

Chapter Thirteen

BECOMING A
"WORLDLY CHRISTIAN"

Did Postmodernism Begin in June 1962?

*W*hen I left Oxford with my family for Winnipeg in 1961, we could not have known how eventful that following summer would be. In June, Russian missiles sailed across the Atlantic to Cuba. For one week, we all thought that the planet might perish in a nuclear holocaust. As the summer began and we started traveling, to the children it was ostensibly a great tour … but for me, I was running away from fear. In retrospect, I think I began to think and live globally during that week. I also think that we might date what we call postmodernism to that very event, which triggered a series of radical changes in Western civilization: the student revolt at the University of Paris in 1969, followed by similar revolts on American campuses against administrative bureaucracy. Hippies began to return to nature, discalced and living among the trees, playing their guitars and living with their girlfriends. They were just carefree young people carrying their parents' Visa cards. There was also a feminist revolt, a sexual revolution, and a new intensity in the rising music culture. In retrospect, all this was a prelude to the creation of Regent College, a reenvisioning of a more radical Christianity.

The phrase of Bonhoeffer's, "being a worldly Christian," relates to Christian stewardship in being responsible citizens of this world, as well as of the world to come. There is evidence that the Cuban missile crisis was at least partly diffused by a well-placed Christian with a personal friendship: As Regent alumnus Michael Tai was to write years later in his book, *U.S.-China Relations in the Twenty-First Century*, one young man, a Sovietologist who had become personal adviser to President Kennedy, strongly advised him that Khruschev would not make a preemptive strike, because he had been a friend of Khruschev's daughter. Often visiting their summer home, he had firsthand experience of Khruschev as an adoring father and grandfather—even as the missiles were sailing across the Atlantic, and Pentagon and State Department officials were urging the president to make a preemptive strike. That young Sovietologist advised President Kennedy: "He won't strike. He is a peaceable man who loves his children and grandchildren. He is a father, and a father will not strike."

That voice may have saved the world, because evidently, President Kennedy listened to him. When a few Christians trust teach other, even though they may be political enemies, they may save the world at a later stage. One young man who knew the Soviet father beforehand helped prevent a catastrophe. What saves the human race? It is personal friendship. And especially Christian personal friendship. Amen!

I was in Washington, DC during another time when personal friendships among potential political enemies, many of whom were Christians even if others were not, helped bring peace in many ways.

New Horizons in Washington, DC: Jim Hiskey

As previously mentioned, I had met Jim Hiskey in 1971 in Jerusalem. In 1973, he invited me to Washington to attend the National Prayer Breakfast. Jim had been a professional golfer; he still mentors golfers, both in the sport and in discipleship. When President Nixon established diplomatic relations with China, playing golf with Chinese leaders became a relaxing ploy, and Jim Hiskey was their teacher on the golf course. He developed remarkable relations, as a Christian, with some of their leaders.

Jim and I agreed in 1973 to begin a series of summer schools at the University of Maryland, which later continued as Summer Studies Institutes at a retreat center near Chesapeake Bay. Having been involved with the creation of Regent College in an academic setting, I realized we could not expect members of the government or the Pentagon, on a four-year rotation, to take a year off from work. Instead, providing a mentor, guided theological reading, occasional evening lectures, and a short summer school could create an appropriate model for taking the Christian faith as seriously and intelligently as one's professional work. The movement is now established in over twenty-five American cities and growing, as well as in Belfast, London, Oxford, Toronto, Vancouver, Tokyo, Singapore, and Dubai, and the Summer Studies Institute gave rise to the C. S. Lewis Institute in 1979.

Washington, DC: The Ku Klux Klansman

A very different friendship was made with Tom Tarrants, who later became President of the C. S. Lewis Institute. I first met Tom after he had been released from prison in 1976, by the advocacy of Charles Colson. Tom (b. 1946) grew up in Mississippi, in a religious home, and, like many others, joined the Ku Klux Klan. This movement, which had begun in the 1860s, has been revived several times. The radical "White Knights of Mississippi" were founded in 1964 as a paramilitary group, and Tom was recruited by Mississippi Wizard Sam Bowers. With two other companions, they plotted to place a bomb under the home of a Jewish businessman, Mayer Davidson, one night. But their group had been infiltrated by the FBI. His companion, Kathy Ainsworth, was killed at the scene. Also shot and bleeding was Tom, but his life was saved by a passing ambulance driver, who heard the shots. After six months in prison, Tom escaped and was recaptured, and was now placed in solitary confinement. Bored, he began to read the Gideon Bible and became aware of a very different faith from what he had grown up with. Eight years later, Tom was released to begin a radically different way of life! He has now published his memoirs.

Washington, DC: The Lost Spade

While visiting Washington in late 1975, I met a fellow Scot, Ernest Gordon, dean of the chapel at Princeton University. He invited me to preach more than once; the first occasion was in March of 1976. He had been an officer in the Argyll and Sutherland Highlanders during World War II. Stationed in Singapore, he tried to flee in a small boat along the Malaysian coast but was captured by the Japanese, and then spent three years in a POW camp. This camp was engaged in building the bridge over the river Kwai, about which a film was made. Although cruelly tortured, he found his faith in Christ there. On one occasion a digging spade was lost, and they were told by the camp commandant that if the spade was not returned they would all be tortured. A Christian prisoner stepped forward and confessed, "I stole it." Immediately he was seized and tortured to death. Soon afterward, the spade was found. Gordon and his companions realized he had saved their lives, as a true martyr. A film, *The Spade*, was later released to tell the story of the brave martyr.

After the war, Ernest earned degrees from London University and Hartford Seminary (Connecticut). He began to preach in local Presbyterian churches and was appointed in 1954 to be dean of the chapel at Princeton. My second visit to that chapel was shared with Charles Colson. All these events have so inspired my own small life!

1978 Sabbatical: A Fruitful Time

Receiving six months' leave from Regent in 1978, I was invited by Dick Halverson, now co-leader of the National Prayer Breakfast, to spend my sabbatical at Fourth Presbyterian Church in Washington. As scholar in residence, I had the opportunity to teach on creation, and out of those lectures I wrote my book *I Believe in the Creator*. Dick wanted me to stay on in Washington, but I knew that I could not be disobedient to what had obviously been a remarkable call of God, to do something rather crazy in Vancouver, with no money—yet—and knowing that other people had not necessarily had that same vision. So I made an excuse to Dick: "You know I have got an allergy."

"Oh?" he said. "What allergy is that?"

"It's an allergy to Potomac Fever. Because of that allergy, I just don't want to get involved in all the politics here."

My wife Rita was mischievous, too: When she saw all these people earnestly talking about going "to the Hill," she used to say, "I have seen a lot of hills in Washington. Which one is *the* hill?"

Of course, they were shocked. How could she be so sacrilegious, when so many people had such an earnest desire for power, for "climbing" Capitol Hill? That summer, we were invited by friends to their lovely home in Long Island, and while we were there, Rita wrote a poem contrasting life on the Hill that makes one breathless with life among the trees or calmly watching the ocean—the liberation that you know when your friends will sit

with you on the beach. She shared my decision to go back to
Vancouver instead of staying in DC.

Washington, DC: Chuck Colson and Prison Fellowship

The Watergate scandal had landed President Nixon's legal
counsel, Charles Colson, in jail. Al Quie—later elected the
governor of Minnesota (1979 to 1983)—befriended Chuck in
prison, and he actually asked the government if he could serve
the rest of Chuck's prison sentence. Al's expression of Christian
love had no precedent in the law courts, but Chuck did win early
release in 1975, after just seven months, due to family issues: his
son had gotten into drug problems. Reading C. S. Lewis's *Mere
Christianity* had convinced Chuck of the truth of Christianity
even before he entered prison. Later, he wrote his book *Born
Again,* and his Prison Fellowship ministries became a worldwide
movement.

I was privileged to accompany Chuck to Al Quie's house in
Minneapolis for a weekend retreat. Later that year, Chuck started
Prison Fellowship. As he began visiting local prisons, I met with
him twice a week for morning Bible studies. He moved fast
and hard, just as he had studied legal briefs, so he was a rather
impatient student of the Bible! Quickly, too, he sought permission
from the head of prison services to try out an experiment in
recidivism.

"Absolutely not," he responded to Chuck, but six months
later he relented after the constant pleas of his own daughter.
Twelve prisoners, including a murderer, and Tom Tarrants, leader
of the C. S. Lewis Institute, whose story is recited later, were
released to a halfway house near Washington for two weeks of
Bible study, teaching, and prayer. Playing baseball for the first
time with this group one Saturday was a new experience for me.
The purpose was to return them to prison as model prisoners,

completing their sentences, to never reoffend. For Chuck, it was simply a way to introduce them to Christ, for he too, had become born again.

Washington, DC: The Beginning of the National Prayer Breakfast Movement

The National Prayer Breakfast, to which Jim Hiskey had invited me in 1973, became a focal point for Washington ministry.

The National Prayer Breakfast movement had arisen in 1942–1943, when a few congressmen and senators had come together to pray about the national dilemma—to remain isolationist or to join Britain, and indeed save Western civilization from defeat against Hitler! Then, a second stage was after a mystical experience General Dwight D. Eisenhower had during the Second World War, after the successful landings in Normandy. He was awakened in the night and felt warned not to take the route he had planned the next day, for he would have been ambushed by superior forces. This saved his life, and his Christian faith was deepened. When he was elected president in 1952, Eisenhower decided to establish a National Prayer Breakfast annually, on the first Friday of February.

It came to the president's attention that Norwegian pastor Abraham Vereide, in Seattle, had organized prayer breakfasts for various groups of business executives, so he invited him to Washington. Then Conrad Hilton offered his hotel in Washington as the locale. President Eisenhower called upon congressmen and senators to take the lead—Republicans and Democrats, united as brothers and sisters in Christ—and the first National Prayer Breakfast was held in 1953.

Then Abraham Vereide, recruited a boy actor in Hollywood, Dick Halverson, who had become ordained as a Presbyterian pastor, and Doug Coe, a Young Life leader, with some other young people to help in the new movement, first to pray, then to disciple others. There was always a feeling that God is going to create a divine synergy at many of the tables in the Hilton for the annual event. This certainly happened to Rita and me in 1978, but that's getting ahead of the story.

Sandra Sharpe, a Lifelong Friend

While Rita and I were in Washington in 1978, Rita volunteered to help with the National Prayer Breakfast, addressing invitations and licking postage stamps for several days. That's where she met Sandra Sharpe (b. 1941). Sandy had taken over the National Prayer Breakfast movement's women's ministry from Barbara Priddy, a woman who created strong rapport with women: at one Bible study, she had the president's wife pouring out her heart. Barbara had a remarkable witness in Washington, and Sandy had big shoes to fill.

Rita met Sandy again in London the next June, when we were celebrating the twenty-fifth wedding anniversary of Rita's sister Grace and her husband Stuart. At the anniversary reception, Rita asked, "Sandy, why don't you come to attend Regent College?"

Sandy did not respond.

Rita added, "The Lord is laying this on my heart."

That was when Sandy remembered a "fleece" she had put before the Lord months before: "Lord, if you want me to go Regent College, please lay this on the Houstons' hearts." As Sandy reported the rest: "The very next night, I received a phone call from my academic advisor. I had vaguely thought this might be my support to enter Regent. Somewhat speechless, I asked if she had received a request from Regent College. No, she hadn't, but she was in town if I wanted to see her. I asked her for a reference … and I was on my way to Regent!"

After nine months at Regent, Sandy continues, "My head was spinning with the richness of my studies, and particularly with a new understanding of the kingdom of God." Instead of returning to her old job, she was offered a staff position in the White House, in the final year of Jimmy Carter's administration. She stayed on for a further two years under President Reagan's administration, in the office of presidential personnel. In 1983–1984, she worked for the National Endowment for the Arts, and in 1985, she was hired by the Department of State, as executive director of the Blair House Restoration Fund for the restoration of Blair House, the president's guest house. Sandy still coordinates all my visits to Washington.

Other Washington Friends

I have had many other wonderful friends in Washington, including Dean Overman and his wife Linda. As a corporate lawyer, previously aide to Nelson Rockefeller in New York, and a White House Fellow, Dean has always worked voluntarily with Young Life. Os Guinness and his wife Jinny have also been lifelong friends; I met them when they were a courting couple at L'Abri, following the Lausanne Conference in 1974. Rich indeed are the friends of Christ. Like so many others, Rita and I have been their beneficiary! Without them, the growth of both Institutes—the C. S. Lewis Institute and Regent College—never could have developed as, by God's mercy, they have.

The Summer Studies/C. S. Lewis Institute

The Summer Studies Institute, which Jim Hiskey and I started formulating in the fall of 1971, was always meant to be an institute of biblical studies for both lay people and those in full-time Christian ministry. At the first Summer Studies Institute in 1976, there were classes taught by John Stott, my friend J. I. Packer, James Montgomery Boice, R. C. Sproul, Senator Mark Hatfield, and Chuck Colson. Other speakers in the early years included Carl Henry, Edmond Clowney, Dick Halverson, Earl Palmer, Norman Geisler, and Os Guinness. The Summer Studies Institute officially became the C. S. Lewis Institute in 1995.

Why change the name? We felt that the new name represented the mission of our institute, not to create a lot of fans for C. S. Lewis, but to nurture ten thousand like him. This would involve engaging with culture, including both political and cultural life, from a boldly Christian approach. We wanted people to take their faith to the same level of competence and intelligence as Lewis.

In Washington, I also met with Bruce MacLaury and his wife Jennie. Bruce was President of Brookings Institution, and he invited Lord Brian Griffith (b. 1941), adviser to Margaret Thatcher, to give a course of lectures on behalf of the C. S. Lewis Institute at Brookings on the necessity of capitalism (a hot topic then and now). He published a book based on his lectures, and later, he became vice-chairman international for Goldman Sachs, and he founded a Christian business school in Romania.

Senator Howard Hughes

Another new relationship was formed at the first Summer Studies Institute at Chesapeake Bay, in 1979. Senator Howard Hughes (1922–1996) had been a truck driver before becoming a Senator in 1969. While despairing of his alcoholism, he became a Christian, and he confessed in a political debate in 1964, "I am an alcoholic and will be till I die ... but with God's help I'll never touch a drop of liquor again." In 1972, widely expected to win the Democratic presidential nomination over George McGovern, he abruptly quit politics to devote the rest of his life to minister to alcoholics. He was subject to depression, and I would sit with him in the garden, trying to encourage him; it helped him to write his autobiography.

Charles Habib Malik

Another distinguished supporter of the C. S. Lewis Institute was Charles Habib Malik (1906–1987), who was an academic diplomat and philosopher who loved Augustine, and gave several courses of lectures on him. He invited me to stay in Beirut at his family home, and to visit the American University of Lebanon, where he had taught. Decorated with honorary doctorates from fifty universities, he was a remarkable Christian voice regarding what a Christian university should be, as in his 1982 book, *A Christian Critique of the University*. I became quite close to him, to comfort him—exiled from his homeland by the civil war, in straitened economic circumstances, and widowed. But like Professor Kis of Budapest, he was lion-hearted in his bold witness for Christ, and he has also inspired me ever since with the depth of his caring.

For many years, I continued to travel to the C. S. Lewis Institute and participate in its Memorial Day retreats at Cedar Point Farm, on Chesapeake Bay. The Institute's programs have been established in many other locales, including Atlanta and Annapolis, Virginia Beach—and in 2016, in Belfast, Northern Ireland, where C. S. Lewis was born.

I have discovered, whether with Regent College or the C. S. Lewis Institute, that when you have ideals for God, other people will also have ideals for God, and God hasn't always coordinated the ideals—and so we sometimes clash, and what started as an ideal becomes politics. And what I have discovered about politics is that politicians don't make personal sacrifices. This means you can often test whether you're teaching theology or political science: in political science, you don't talk about personal sacrifice—but when you're talking about theology and the work of the kingdom of God, inevitably you are talking about personal sacrifices.

Chapter Fourteen

MY CONFIDANTE,
ERNST VAN EEGHEN

Memoirs of the Cold War

*A*t the National Prayer Breakfast in February 1978, at the
Hilton Hotel, we were invited to host a table, and a Dutch
couple, Ernst (1920–2007) and Erika van Eeghen (d. 1984),
joined us there. It's a good thing we didn't realize that Erika was a
French baroness, cousin of Giscard d'Estaing, president of France,
or that Ernst was CEO of the oldest family trading company
in the Netherlands! His family's original ships were the flying
clippers that brought spices, teas, and coffees from Dutch East
India, and then—as the world changed—the family was part of
a consortium that bought millions of acres of land around "New
Amsterdam" (central and western New York state, and western
Pennsylvania) and began to sell or rent it out. Rita would have
had a fit if she knew all that when she met them; she was always
scared of dignitaries. But on that night, she only knew that a
lovely, humble sister in Christ wanted to speak with her about the
Lord.

During table talk, we mentioned our summer school at Regent College, and although Ernst seemed somewhat distant, Erika said she would love to have someone teach her about the psalms. They came to Regent that very summer. They both were deeply blessed by the lecture course taught by Bruce Waltke on the psalms, and Ernst was radically changed. He became a devout Christian as well. Thus began a long, close friendship, with visits to their home "Berkenrode" in Heemstede, north of Amsterdam, and to their summer chalet at "Uhu" in Wengen, in the Swiss Alps. I was deeply privileged to have a long, remarkable correspondence with Ernst; I remember that he told me he had been a very lonely man, and that he was so thankful he could share so many secrets with me. As in John Innes's beautiful poem about his own loneliness, "Re-Discovered by My Constant Lover," that lonely man became a glorious we! He entrusted me with many confidential letters that only recently resurfaced in my home; they will have to be filed for another generation to write the full story of all that happened at Ernst's instigation during a major crisis in world history. Still, here are a few highlights from our correspondence.

We first corresponded about creating an institute similar to Regent College, but in Europe—and about Ernst's financial support of the C. S. Lewis Institute in Washington. Then he began to send me copies of correspondence he had, from 1978 onwards, with Soviet and American leaders, trying to defuse the Cold War. Ernst had been severely wounded in the Second World War, which left him with 60 percent mobility and energy for the rest of his life, and which necessitated two or three operations each year for some time. When he and I first corresponded, he still was having these operations to deal with his crippled feet; he could walk, but it took courage, since he was always in pain.

Queen Wilhelmina (Queen of the Netherlands, 1890–1948) had appointed him honorary president of the Dutch Veterans Association after World War II, and he helped fund the formation of the Association of European Churches. As vice-president of that Association's budget committee, he became a trusted friend of the Orthodox Patriarch of Russia, Alexy II, a friendship that lasted for some twenty-five years.

Around 1978, concerned that we might face a nuclear holocaust unless there was an open line for private communication between Soviet and American leaders, he thought, "Why don't I knock at the door of the president of the veterans association of the Soviet Union?" He reached out to Semion Ivanov in a letter, and later he discovered—I'm not sure whether it was in glee or in fear—that he had contacted a KGB general.

Nevertheless, he invited General Ivanov to visit his and Erika's spacious home in Heemstede. There, one midnight when the general's security guard (undoubtedly a spy) was in bed, the general broke all protocol and knocked gently at Ernst and Erika's bedroom door.

"Erika," he told her, "you remind me of my beloved grandmother, who was also a devoted Christian."

Now, they shared the intimacy of confidence in peril of their lives. That was the nature of Soviet friendship—someone who holds your life in his or her hands. You only dared to have two or three of this kind of friend. They began to communicate discreetly, and this man secretly became a Christian himself.

On another visit, he asked Ernst if he could procure a new cancer drug to save his wife's life. Ernst was able to help, and later, Ernst asked for a return favor. Baptist pastor Vladimir Khailo, along with his elder son, had been imprisoned and was being "treated" (experimented on, with mind-changing drugs) for "religious schizophrenia." Would General Ivanov try to have them released? The general groaned, knowing he might be endangering his career, but he promised to do his best. Several of Pastor Khailo's daughters were unmarried, but once it was made public that the family would be released to go to the West, those unmarried daughters very soon found suitors and married. Pastor Khailo was let out of prison, and with his newly expanded family, he was allowed to leave the Soviet Union. Eventually— after having been quarantined in Friesland, the Netherlands, for six months in 1986—he and his family were admitted to the United States.

In the meantime, Ernst's correspondence shows his involvement in helping communications flow during power shifts in the Soviet Union, with its missile threats to western Europe, as power shifted away from Brezhnev, whom he felt was a man of peace. The great issue of the day was the installation of nuclear missiles in western Europe, which made European countries potential targets for Soviet nuclear missiles. Ernst worked tirelessly to try to decrease the nuclear threat.

To protect the families of the Soviet delegates now mentioned by Ernst van Eeghen, I have designated them in sequence: A, B, C, and D. Likewise, under US security measures, the American delegates are not named.

At one meeting, A told Ernst, "When I'm in Moscow, I always feel the presence of the Lord and the devil much closer than anywhere else in the world." But when he came to Heemstede and breathed fresh air and friendship, with no fear of the enemy, it was like a sabbatical. "When you are in prayer"— this is the testimony of a Soviet leader, a secret Christian!—"God does amazing things."

Ernst traveled the world, including many trips to Moscow and Washington. He and Erika also spent twelve years in Tanganyika, representing the family business. There, they became friends of my sister-in-law, Sheila Davidson, and her husband, Arthur Scotchmere—and of President Nyere, united in trying to stamp out corruption in African trade. Ernst sent me memoranda of extensive tours to China, Siberia, and the Ukraine, as an astute businessman who could see all the potentials of their national resources. He facilitated Dutch Agricultural Advisory Reform Aid, helping to develop a large sector of land in the Ukraine. But his most amazing achievements were the facilitating of high-level informal talks between the Soviets and the Americans, especially concerning the nuclear missiles. He made two interesting things clear to me about those talks: first, that he had not initiated them himself; and second, that it was discouraging that the Americans involved were so ultra-cautious about participating. He felt that this was ironic, for they had little to lose if the secret negotiations broke down, while the Soviet negotiators were risking their lives.

A key role in the secret talks was played by A. P. Shitikov, president of the Supreme Soviet, who first visited Ernst at Berkenrode in March, 1982. Frankly, he told Ernst, it was dumb to be an atheist and a communist! He had once been a nominal Orthodox Christian, but as he began reading the Bible for himself, he became convinced of its truth, becoming a strong Christian. As the secret conference was being planned, it was Shitikov who suggested three delegates for both sides—Russian and American—be nominated by each country. With their interpreters and aides, twelve residents attended the "Berkenrode Consultation" in 1984.

B, vice-president of the Soviet Committee for European Security and Co-operation, whom Ernst knew from 1981, was also a consistent friend and a man of peace. At one point, B frankly told Ernst that the aim of Mr. Gromyko was to split Western Europe from the United States, so he was "terrifying the United States not to have missiles [in western Europe], so where are we in this terrible mess?" He asked Ernst about his motive for being involved in these matters. Ernst replied that he had no political or financial motives whatsoever, no other motive than simply being a Christian. B believed him, for he was acting out of the same Christian motive.

During the week of the National Prayer Breakfast in 1983, I invited Ernst and a few other friends to dine at the Cosmos Club, where I was a member. Afterwards, the manager of the club came to me rather shamefacedly, asking me for the names of my dinner guests.

"You know the protocol better than I do," I said.

"No, not at all!"

Afterward, I told Ernst that perhaps the FBI was trailing him. "They're probably in cahoots with the KGB."

He laughed, saying, "You are scared of these KGB people. I'm not the slightest bit scared about the KGB. Why should I be afraid, when I am already a friend of a KGB general?"

It became clear in about 1983 that Leonid Brezhnev, the president of the Soviet Union, who had been "a man of peace," was dying. Gromyko, who favored confrontation, had not yet been elected (he had many enemies), but he held the reins of power for a critical six weeks between January and late February of 1983. During that time, those who were more peaceable gradually, inched forward, trying to gain influence for peace. It's a remarkable moment that is not recorded in history at all, largely because it has been buried under the Secret Service Act of the United States—but I can, of course, share my personal memories about a man who gave me copies of numerous documents: a copy of the Warsaw Pact, a copy of principles for transitioning from SHAEF to NATO, and many others. The demand for neutrality was strident throughout Europe in the 1980s. Many people did not want nuclear missiles in Europe at all. Ernst was told that nobody knew where Gromyko stood, that all the leaders were in a state of fear of each other, not knowing who would make the first move, since the first move could expose you to terrible danger. Gromyko was well aware that some channel of communication had been opened up through the Netherlands, and he was pressuring the head of the Russian foreign office to require all contacts to work through the Soviet foreign office. Meanwhile, the Russians felt greatly threatened by China. If China were to side with the United States against Russia in a confrontation, that could be a great plus for the Americans.

B, Gromyko's close friend, described himself to Ernst as being "heavily overworked," as a leader of a world power, compared with Ernst in a small country. B said, "It was a hard time to think, a hard time to have pity on your enemy; the danger facing everyone with Gromyko was that he will have the instinct of a wolf, not the instincts of a man. And when a man is so overwrought with fear that he becomes like a bear, an angry bear, he believes it's only instincts that help him survive. In our world today," B continued, "we have no idea of that kind of a person— but that's the kind of person who was living in those days."

During this time, Ernst was realizing that he could trust the generals in a way that he could not trust politicians. The military men were "jolly good fellows" who would drink with him and laugh with him about their wounds; they shared a comradeship that no political scientist could understand, never having been wounded.

Billy Graham went to Moscow during the Cold War, and when Ernst told him about his Russian friends, Billy (somewhat naively) said that he was "being deceived by the devil."

Ernst was convinced otherwise: "Yes, we know the severity of God, but we know the severity of his mercy."

Ernst told me that in the beginning, Billy used Ernst's relationship with the Orthodox Patriarch to help set up his evangelistic campaign in Moscow—but then he repeatedly brushed aside any advice or channels of communication that Ernst tried to give him for his Moscow rally. Largely as a result, Billy got the cold shoulder from the patriarch—as if to say "We are a Christian community here already. Who do you think you are, coming here to say that we are not Christians?" Sadly, Billy Graham's campaign in Moscow accomplished less than it might have.

For example: C, Deputy Director (second in command) of the Soviet Institute of USA and Canada Studies, also communicated regularly with Ernst. In September 1983, Ernst recounted this conversation to me. "C asked me why I invested so much time and money in my efforts since the last fifteen months to get the Americans and the Soviets together. Did I expect to be refunded by the Soviet Government? ... I answered him that I did not expect any money from anyone and would not accept it if it were offered me. As a Christian, however, I felt that in these apocalyptic times it was important to do whatever possible to get the two parties together. Official talks had failed [for] nearly forty years, and the stockpile of nuclear arms had increased on both sides at a scale [where] nobody could have the faintest idea of what this really meant.... Then C looked me straight in the face and said that he too was a Christian. He had been converted during the visit of Billy Graham to Moscow.... that Dr. Graham was the strongest and most exceptional man he had ever met."

Ernst continued, "I asked [Rodomir] how he could combine his Christian faith and Marxism. He answered that this was not difficult if you only left away the atheist part of Marxism. The communist and capitalist systems were in fact not important. They were changing all the time, and of both very good things and very bad things could be said. It was the hearts of the people that mattered. The changing of the systems would take time, and neither he nor anyone else could change them overnight.... We left it at that. But I clearly felt I had gained one more friend in the Soviet world."

C assured Ernst at a later meeting, "I am still very much a Christian." He wished Ernst "God's blessing, very, very much, because I too undoubtedly need this." He also said that he too envied Ernst because he was a citizen of a very small country. Representing a superpower, he said, "is almost impossible, the problems are much greater than any human being can cope with." This human cry should remind all Christians of the appeal of the apostle, to pray "for kings and all that are in authority" (1 Tim 2:2).

On September 8, 1986, Ernst wrote me: "We are obviously living in a most dangerous nuclear time. The Lord is, however, giving us extraordinary chances to form the growing Christian international society on which eventually HIS Kingdom on earth will be built. Nobody knows how, [or] how long it will take, but we should be ready to use every possibility. Otherwise we will fail our Lord Jesus Christ. This has no relationship whatsoever to the national security of a country … We all know what happened in 1939 after the preceding years of compromise. A war invalid like me is daily reminded …You might want to keep out of all this, if so, I can fully appreciate your attitude as the whole thing must be quite foreign to you."

On another occasion, depressed by all these pressures, he advised me to get rid of all our correspondence. Instead, I left them all quite forgotten in our basement, only to be recovered and remembered in February 2018.

Ernst also organized a Human Rights International Conference, held in 1991, at which Mrs. Rosalynn Carter and Madame Giscard d'Estaing were chief speakers. He further tried to establish a Commission on International Corruption, in view of his own business trading in East Africa.

On May 28, 1992, Ernst was a signatory, as secretary to American and British representatives, in a statement advising Russian President Yeltsin and Ukranian President Kravchuk in talks to remove tactical nuclear weapons from the Ukraine. Such was the confidence that was given to a Christian from a small nation, for his services as a "worldly Christian." Dietrich Bonhoeffer coined that phrase, and Ernst van Eeghen was an outstanding exemplar. His personal motto was "A Christian Must Work Toward Peace," and using his singular position to great advantage, he encouraged many key political and military leaders, Russian and American, to save us from a nuclear holocaust. As I said, his full story has still to be told.

Soviet Generals Whom Ernst Knew, Many as Friends

Ernst's friendship with Soviet generals was pivotal, since they generally were men of peace—unlike some of the politicians. Because their military positions remained more secure than those of the politicians, they could take risks and initiate negotiations. Ernst mentioned the following names to me very often. C, a KGB general, general of the Veterans Association, was later vice-chairman of the Institute of US and Canadian Studies. He also knew Colonel General Iwanov Maryesev, the most decorated hero of the Soviet Union and a household name. As a Soviet ace fighter pilot in World War II, he had lost both legs, and Ernst visited him in hospital whenever he was in Moscow. He also often mentioned Colonel General Viktor Chernov, Lieutenant General Baatov, and his predecessor in the Praesidium of the Military Generals, Lieutenant General Ivanov. As a political friend once wrote to Ernst, "There is no relationship given that does not have a future purpose."

A Personal Portrait of E. H. van Eeghen

I never could have imagined that Ernst should want so intimately to be my friend. Why me? A few quotes from his letters to me provide an intimate personal portrait.

When his mother died, he wrote to me back on April 1, 1981:

> ... the death of my mother is indeed a great loss, as I was always very attached to her. She taught me the Christian life since I was a baby, and gave a perfect example [in] herself. She stood for what she said, and during the war—when she hid during more than four years three Jews, under very difficult circumstances—her acts proved to confirm her words. My mother never hesitated, and once she made up her mind, she stuck to it whatever the consequences could be. Apart from that, she was always loving and never carried any hate towards anybody. Before she died, she told me that she was sure that she would enter a new and better world and meet again my father and elder brother.
>
> The past year has not really been very hard on me. I do undergo every two months a small operation

regarding my war wounds, and I am getting accustomed to it and they are much less painful than at the beginning....

When he came with Erica to our Summer School at Regent College in 1979, Erika wrote to Rita and myself,

> ... our stay at Regent has been one of the most wonderful experiences we have ever had. I cannot tell you how grateful we have been for this opportunity, and we really feel it has been a tremendous encouragement in our spiritual life. I do hope the seeds that were sown there have sunk in good soil with not too many thistles and weeds ...

I believe that the soil was good indeed.

The day after Erica's sudden death in 1984, Ernst found tucked in her Bible his "marching orders," which she had written two years before. He wrote about it to me:

> A new life has started for me, a new world, where I must eat and pray. Erika will be watching me. I feel her hand on me.... I am on the right road, and at the end of the road, there will be Erica and together we will kneel before Christ. Could I ever have anything more beautiful? ... I hope you can read my still-shaky handwriting. It is past midnight and our house is silent....
> Love in Christ,
> Yours, Ernst

Those "marching orders" from Erika were written in her own hand:

> In all my prayers for all of you, I always pray with joy because of your partnership in the Gospel from the first day until now, being confident of this, that he who began a good work in you will carry it on to completion until the day of Jesus Christ (Phil 1:4–6 NIV).
>
> But one thing I do: Forgetting what is behind and straining toward what is ahead, I press onward to the goal to win the prize for which God has called me heavenward in Christ Jesus (Phil 3:13, 14 NIV).

Rejoice in the Lord always. I will say it again: Rejoice! Let your gentleness be known to everyone. The Lord is near. Be not anxious about anything, but in prayer and petitions and thanksgiving, present your request to God. And the peace of God which transcends all understanding will guard your minds in Christ Jesus (Phil 4:4–7).

Do everything without complaining or arguing, so that you may become blameless and pure, children of God without fault in a crooked and depraved generation, in which you shine like stars in the universe as you hold onto the word of life (Phil 2:14–16a NIV).

I can do everything through Him who gives me strength (Phil 4:13 NIV).

Ernst had so won the heart of General Georgi Arbatov (president of the Russian Institute of US and Canada Studies) and his wife Svetlana, that when Erica died he wrote to Ernst on November 17, 1984:

> Dear Ernst,
>
> I cannot thank you enough for your moving letter and a beautiful candle holder, which we shall cherish in remembrance of our dear Erica, whom I and Svetlana loved so much, and who will always be in our hearts.
>
> We fully relish the gravity of your loss and the tormenting grief that has descended on you. We shall always cherish our beloved gone, but life goes on and you owe to Erika's memory to take care of yourself and stay active, which is the only way to survive this tragedy. Besides, think of all the people and causes which still need you. Imagine what would happen to this world if all the honorable and able withdraw into themselves?
>
> We also need you, Ernst, and do hope that you have the strength and courage needed to hold on through this ordeal.
>
> With kindest regards also from Svetlana,
> Ever yours,
> Georgi Arbatov

These are words for us all.

Chapter Fifteen

LIVING AS A
"WORLDLY CHRISTIAN"

Visit to Romania, December 1990

One of my son Christopher's friends, Chris Shore, was a senior
executive with World Vision in Toronto. I had occasional links
with World Vision, beginning with a Brazilian friend, Valdir
Steuernagel, who first was its head in Brazil, and then later
served as chair of World Vision's board and vice-president of
Christian Commitments. He invited me to attend a National
Interdenominational Call to Repentance of various church
leaders at Iasi, capital of Romania's East Moldovia region. The
intention was to publicly confess their lack of concern for the
millions of children who had been experimented upon by the
dictator Nicolae Ceausescu, in his attempts to create "Socialist
Man"; many country priests had actually been complicit with the
experiment, and had recruited peasant children. These peasants
had been assured their children would have a glorious new life,
as wards of the court (or of the state), but instead, they were
placed in barracks-like quarters in small cots and denied tender
loving care. As a result, they were permanently brain damaged.

Unaware of the damage and its permanent implications, after the dictator's fall World Vision sent hundreds of these children to the United States for adoption by unsuspecting parents. This lasted until 2006, when it was acknowledged how seriously damaged the children were. To this day, Romania has more ward-of-court children and young people than any other country.

I was one of four plenary speakers at the conference, representing the evangelical churches alongside heads of the Greek and Russian Orthodox, Roman Catholic, and Romanian evangelical churches. It was a unique event in my life! Beforehand, I was invited to visit the city of Timisoara on Romania's western border with Hungary, where the Romanian revolution had begun. My guide on that occasion, who also organized other visits, was Danut Manastireanu, the Romanian World Vision leader.

As Danut explained to me, the inhabitants of the Western Border saw hope that no other part of Romania ever could, because of its access to western television: that in one extraordinary year, the Berlin Wall had fallen, Kosovo had become independent from Serbia, and Hungary was free. I was actually invited to preach at the Baptist church in Str. Cezar Boliac, at which the revolution had begun, and the pastor—Reverend Petru Dugulescu—explained what had happened on the date of the infamous Timisoara Massacre.

He had never had political intentions; he had simply sought for his congregation to have a spiritual revival. So after the Sunday evening service on December 16, he had led his congregation out onto the street leading to the central square, and every thousand steps, they would all kneel on the street and publicly recite the Lord's Prayer. He took me on that same walk and pointed out where a young woman had been shot—where the Sunday school leader had fallen—and related that there had been several hundred casualties in a very short distance. Dum-dum bullets were used by the troops, bullets that expand in the brain or body, creating such bloody carnage that the bloodstains still were visible a year later. I saw them as I passed down the street. One memorable moment was when a young pastor paused and pointed out, "This is where my fiancé was shot, as we walked arm in arm!" Eventually the troops, nauseated by such cruelty, refused to keep shooting and actually joined the procession. Close to the main city center, factory workers poured out onto the street. By the time the concourse had reached the main square, the city's mayor had fled. Ascending through the town hall, the pastor appeared on the balcony, bravely prepared to be shot, but calling on all the concourse to fall on their knees and say, yet again, the Lord's Prayer (the fact that this use of the Lord's Prayer was never reported by the press only showed the strong reaction against religious reporting). In one major city after the other, the revolution was triggered—with much less bloodshed by now, for the whole army had revolted. Most of the thousand deaths occurred there in Timisoara.

On December 22, Nicolae Ceausescu fled from the palace in Bucharest in a helicopter, but his personal pilot turned traitor and landed near a police station, making the excuse that he had to refuel. Ceausescu was arrested and taken back to the palace, and on that same day, he was tried, sentenced to death, and shot along with his wife Elena, ending one of the cruelest dictatorships on record.

Visits to the Caucasian Republics, 1991–1993

I was also invited by World Vision to pay two visits to Armenia. The first was to hold a week's retreat for their staff workers in the spring of 1991. Because of the need to develop micro-management in a country whose economy needed radical reform, over half of the World Vision team in Armenia were not Christians. The purpose of the retreat was for me to explain what it means to be "a Christian." I was inspired by meeting the retired

"Catholicos" or primate of the Armenian Church, who had been one of some forty students when Stalin permitted their seminary to reopen in 1943. But as he told me, as we sat facing each other across his office table, he was left with only a handful of clergy four years later; the others could not endure the persecution. Truly he was a selfless, godly man. He had quietly resigned in order to allow one of his pupils to reign, to sustain the future leadership. To me it was a unique moment of self-sacrificial love in the cause of Christ.

Alas, I have forgotten his name—but he conducted me to the ancient cathedral some sixty kilometers from Yereven, the Armenian capital. He personally took me behind the high altar, down some ancient steps and at the floor level of the raised dais, and pointed out the crude rubble stonework under the high altar; it was not Christian, but Zoroastrian. Clearly, we could trace the outline of the red-fired clay vessel that had held the sacred fire. Like many Christian churches built over Roman temples, here was the same imagery: Christ as conqueror over pagan worship. As a geographer interested in the origins of cultivated plants, I also realized that probably the origin of the olive was here in the Caucasus, where the Zoroastrians had held sacred the very olive oil that burned in the sacred fire.

I had the privilege, at the university in Yereven, to lecture in the building that had been the old Institute of Atheism (under Soviet rule), and was now the Armenian Institute of Christian Studies. Quite a reversal! Still, the legacy of the Soviet Empire was apparent in the giant chemical factory rusting away in the northern suburb, built when the Soviet economic policy had been to maintain such specialized plants in the whole of the Soviet Union. Another grim reminder of the tragic history of Armenia: maps were being sold in street stalls, depicting the millions of deaths in the genocide perpetrated by the Turks from 1915–1919. Although Turkey has acknowledged this crime, it is still a cause of great political tension between the two countries. Armenia also has ongoing tensions with its neighboring state of Azerbaijan, since a splinter of mountains between them is claimed by both states.

A year after the independence of Georgia in 1991, I was invited by InterVarsity to lead a retreat in the mountains outside Tiflis, the capital. At the camp, I met the Georgian (and also world!) champion of wrestling. Why, I asked, were Georgians and Japanese so often the world wrestling champions? My friend explained that it was simply because these two countries were hemmed in and could not afford to lose any more territory. Likewise in wrestling, oftentimes losing a few inches of ground is to lose the match. I also visited the town of Gorky, where there is a museum containing the train compartment where Stalin signed the Yalta Treaty with the Western powers. The curator, thinking I was a loyal communist, invited me to sit in Stalin's seat on the train! I ruminated, then, how strange that one Georgian seminary student should become the terror who was Stalin, while another Georgian, a Christian, Secretary of State Shevardnadze, should have held Christian retreats with James A Baker III, the US Secretary of State, to break up the Soviet Empire!

The Anti-Apartheid Movement of South Africa

Some years back, I had been invited by Michael Cassidy (b. 1936), whom I had met at Fuller Seminary in Pasadena, to speak at a Conference of Reconciliation in Pietermaritzburg. This began a series of visits to South Africa, including one in which I was the plenary speaker in Johannesburg at the Presbyterian Church in South Africa. It was inspiring, during one visit, to meet privately at the home of the moderator of the Afrikaans Church, Professor Johan Adam Heyns. He had dared to challenge the apartheid mentality of his own church, and he was assassinated shortly afterward, in 1994. His assassin(s) was (were) never identified.

On another occasion, Trevor Hudson, then pastor of Northfield Methodist Church in Benoni, South Africa, invited me to stay at his home. I was warned never to stop at a red light intersection, but to gradually drive towards it, and anticipate the green light. To stop could easily be to be seized on by a gang of youths. The youth of South Africa were a "fatherless generation," whose fathers worked as gold and diamond miners, often thousands of miles away and returning home perhaps only one week annually. Another mark of lawlessness: I watched Trevor take ten minutes to bolt the inside and outside doors of his house, as well as his garage. All suburban residents lived in such "fortresses."

Visiting the vast slums by day with local Christian residents was much safer. I also was privileged to visit the high-rise home of the Catholic order of "the Little Brothers/Sisters" of Charles de Foucault, who see themselves like the Desert Fathers of early Christianity, now living in the urban desert of modern alienation. I have many memories of wonderful friendships with courageous Christians in South Africa, fighting *apartheid*, including John Reid, pro- then vice-chancellor of the University of Cape Town, and Rory Prest, a leader of the InterVarsity movement, both of whom came to Regent College as students.

Back in Canada, where politicians were banning the import of South African goods, the new South African ambassador requested early on in his appointment to be permitted to visit Native Canadian settlements. He saw the hypocrisy of apartheid also being practiced in Canada!

Major General J. S. Grinalds: The Rest of the Story

I have mentioned that John S. Grinalds, the Rhodes scholar at Brasenose College, was not yet a Christian while at Oxford, but that he had accepted Christ as his Lord in a foxhole in Vietnam— and that he later led Oliver North to Christ.

Grinalds was appointed deputy general to SHAEF, the precursor of NATO—then he was appointed Major General in charge of all ground forces in the United States, in case of nuclear war. In 1991, his superior officers were investigating whether he should be further promoted, when they learned he attended a Thursday evening Bible study with Oliver North, who then was embroiled in the Iran arms scandal. Grinalds was told he could not be considered for advancement unless he stopped seeing North. Out of loyalty to his friend, he indignantly retired from the US Marine Corps and took the humble position of a headmaster of a private boys' school, Woodberry Forest in Virginia.

Five years later, he was recalled by the Pentagon and appointed president of the Citadel, the southern equivalent of West Point (1997–2005). Women's integration had been straightforward in the Army, the Navy, and the Air Force, but the intense male bonding of the Marines made this another matter! John spoke of how a Marine would travel a thousand miles to help a buddy—and here I choked, remembering how two of our first Regent College students had done just that in late August, 1970, and had been killed on their thousand-mile journey to attend a fellow Marine's wedding in Texas. Now it was John's task to try and accomplish women's integration at the Citadel. In his acceptance speech, he spoke to an audience of over 5,000, saying he had been blessed by many mentors, but beyond them all was Jesus Christ. It was one of the best moments of my life!

He concluded his address thusly: "I finally came to the conclusion that the greatest example of good leadership, servant leadership, is that practiced by Jesus Christ. The New Testament is full of examples of his caring. He included everyone in his service. No one was rejected. He understood what was deep in the heart of an individual and was always faithful in his ministry to the need he saw there. He sacrificed everything, including his life, to meet the needs of those by his side and, in fact, for all mankind for all time. That's what people hope for in their leaders: care, understanding, and sacrifice. What more can we ask than that the graduates of this venerable institution move into society, filled with care, understanding, and the willingness to sacrifice all in their service of mankind . . . May God help us all in this endeavor. *Semper fidelis*."

Chapter Sixteen

BOOK PUBLISHING AND THE MINDSET OF LANDSCAPE STUDIES

I have often been asked, What does being a geographer have to do with getting involved in a theological college? I answer: Not much, if you are a geomorphologist (interpreting the interplay of geology and the physical landscape). But as a cultural geographer (a historian of ideas) trained in air-photographic interpretation, the interplay of history in differing cultures, and having a mind trained to synthesize, it makes much more sense. A mathematician tends to be skeptical about all reality, while a painter or a poet trusts in personal intuition. And a Christian, especially one who inherited "basic trust" as a child, can transcend all mind-sets. More of a confession than a memoir, then, is this section about my teaching and books—beginning while I was teaching at Oxford and continuing up to the time of writing this memoir.

With my Oxford students, we frequently discussed what it means to be a "Christian geographer." A few of my alumni still meet periodically for that purpose! My *magnum opus* as a geographer was the university textbook published in 1964, *The*

Western Mediterranean World: An Introduction to Its Regional Landscapes. Ironically for a superpower, education in the United States has been weak on geography, in contrast to the Soviet Union and European countries. A brave effort was made by geographers at the Universities of Chicago and California in the early 1960s, but it failed to change school curricula. For me, then, publishing on diverse world landscapes was a cause, not just a career.

I was asked by the publisher of my university text to edit a whole series of books, which continued to flow long after I had left Oxford: *China* (1969), *The Soviet Union* (1969), *Ireland* (1970), *New Zealand* (1970), *Terrain Evaluation* (1973), *Australia* (1975), *France* (1975), *Japan* (1976), *Brazil* (1982), *Nigeria* (1983), *Italy* (1983), and *Eastern Europe* (1985). Most of the thirteen authors were natives of the countries they wrote about. At the time this series began to release, I was also supervising doctoral students working in the troubled political areas of El Salvador, the Santa Marta region of Northern Colombia, and in Costa Rica; all in the 1970s, when Regent College was still somewhat of a "troubled territory" itself.

Books and the Shaping
of a Program in Christian Studies

Early on in Vancouver, despite my income-generating work at UBC, my main focus remained at Regent College, and the new things we were doing there. People used to tease me, knowing my background in geography, that I must have come to Regent to study the landscape of the soul! There was truth in that: reviewing knowledge in synthesis, rather than by analysis, had become my métier. But in a hyper-cognitive world (even of evangelical leaders), it was not a popular approach! Your mind "mattered" more than your heart, especially for evangelical leaders who did not realize they were still under the hyper-cognitive influence of the "age of reason." But I was already in revolt against teaching the reductionism of "systematic theology," and so we introduced "spiritual theology" into the Regent curriculum from the start. Some were suspicious of my orthodoxy, as I encountered from Francis Schaeffer and even my friend John Stott, who later wrote *The Christian Mind*. Further, the idea of a layman in theological studies who claimed "the priesthood of all believers" (i.e., Plymouth Brethren thinking) sounded very suspicious to some of our local clergy. Like C. S. Lewis, we were claiming to be "mere Christians." But my links with Spanish Conciliar theologians had stimulated me to try and introduce spiritual theology into evangelical scholarship. Also, from a distance, my family friend Tom Torrance's generous gift of his lecture notes on Christian dogmatics helped steer the new program.

For texts for my new surveys on "the landscape of the soul," I began to teach on church reformers (especially the Christian mystics), using their own writings. I thought that to make them more contemporary to an audience who was historically "stuck" with the Protestant Reformation, I should invite contemporary Christian leaders to write introductions, explaining why these texts were relevant to their own thinking and ministry. Multnomah Press, in Portland, Oregon, agreed to run the series. Appropriately, Senator Mark Hatfield of Oregon agreed to write an introduction for the first volume, William Wilberforce's text on *Real Christianity: Contrasted with the Prevailing Religious System*, in 1982 (I had become a friend of Mark Hatfield at the National Prayer Breakfast movement). My colleague Jim Packer, as a Puritan "fan," introduced John Owen's *Sin and Temptation* in 1983. Dick Halverson, as Chaplain to the US Senate, introduced Richard Baxter's *The Reformed Pastor* in 1985, and later, he also wrote an introduction for Owen's *Communion with God*.

In my travels to Latin America, I had become a friend of Clayton L. Berg, Director of the Latin American Mission. With considerable moral courage, he agreed to introduce Teresa of

Avila's *A Life of Prayer*, and her classic, *The Interior Castle* (1983). Because of Leon Morris's writings on the cross of Christ, on a visit to Australia I asked him to introduce some figures quite unknown to him, but whom he was willing to explore: Juan de Valdes and Don Benedetto's *The Benefit of Christ: Living Justified Because of Christ's Death* (1984). Meanwhile my friendship with Charles Colson had ripened, and though always very busy, he agreed to introduce Jonathan Edwards's *Religious Affections: How Man's Will Affects His Character Before God* (1984). A visiting professor at Regent, David Jeffrey (then based at Victoria University, BC), offered to introduce the fourteenth-century mystic Walter Hilton's *Toward A Perfect Love* in 1985. Os Guinness was an old friend who chose to introduce Blaise Pascal's *The Mind on Fire: An Anthology ... including the Pensees* (1989). My old friend John Stott agreed to introduce *Evangelical Preaching: An Anthology of Sermons by Charles Simeon* (1986).

By this time, the small Oregon publisher was getting alarmed that our ever-expanding series would monopolize their need for a balanced book list. Amicably, we agreed to end the series. But this series sparked a new interest among evangelicals in America, where "Christian history" had not been a strong educational focus. What was becoming a cultural norm was psychology and psychotherapy, and to this norm, I now began to pay attention—for I remained keenly committed to mentoring, from my tutorial heritage at Oxford.

I had already published *I Believe in the Creator* (1980), at the invitation of my colleague Michael Green, for his "I Believe" series. Then I had written *Prayer, the Transforming Friendship* (1989), which was published by David Alexander, an old Oxford friend. Financially stretched too far by expanding into the American market, his publishing house launched our hardcover book at just the wrong time, and it ended up stacked in the warehouse of Cook Communications in Colorado. By chance, fourteen years later, the book reemerged, thanks to a passing glance from the CEO, who read it—and it changed his life, as he later told me. It was then reissued by various publishers, each retitling the book to their fancy, and finally it was rescued by Regent Publishing and restored to its original title.

Later books had a more conventional journey. In 1990, a contemporary study of the enneagram was used to explore *In Search of Happiness: A Guide to Personal Contentment*. Then in 1992, we published *The Heart's Desire: A Guide to Personal Fulfillment*, illustrating various icons of the history of the church: the martyr, the desert father, the Cistercian "garden of the soul," the medieval pilgrim, and the contemporary "child of God." Probing into how early Christianity began as a movement of letter writing, I then launched a quest to select 365 letters, one for each day of the year, to celebrate the saints' feast days in more sacramental meditation. This was entitled *Letters of Faith through the Seasons* (2006). Writers ranged through the whole history of the church, from précis of the New Testament writers, then letters throughout history, to contemporary writers. One of the most moving was from a Jewish Christian Holocaust survivor, a psychiatrist in Budapest. It took her three years to write, for first she had to join a Lutheran choir in Budapest, knowing that when the choir toured Germany, some in the audience would be Nazi guards from the death camps, and she was singing forgiveness to them! They were costly letters to write. Indeed, I have never witnessed such widespread explorations into the human soul as these letters revealed to me personally.

The same year, 2006, I wrote a veiled autobiography, *Joyful Exiles: Life on the Dangerous Edge of Things*. For in church one Sunday morning, months before, I had preached on what I thought I was called by the Lord to begin, "a hidden life in Christ." That is why I now struggle to write these memoirs. I saw all too clearly the vanity, indeed the idolatry, of much Christian ministry and scholarship. I have never seen myself as a writer, perhaps because of my early Regent colleague Bill Martin, who had become too paralyzed to publish anything. He had dared to critique an article by G. R. Driver, son of the great Old Testament scholar Samuel R. Driver, and the father determined Bill's work would not be published. In sharp contrast, our mutual friend F. F. Bruce had poured out commentary after commentary, reading galley proofs as he commuted each day to Manchester University. Ruefully, Bill condemned Bruce as "drowning himself in printer's ink." I suspect I was afraid of meeting a like fate—so it was better not to be "a writer," but just to go on writing!

Then the Lord used my beloved friend and colleague, Bruce Waltke, to invite me to collaborate with him on his commentary on select psalms. It is a tribute to Bruce's textual skills, as a Hebraic scholar; my contribution has been as a historian of ideas, contributing receptive exegesis—how a psalm might have been interpreted and preached within a specific period of history. Like no other assignment, these studies have deepened my soul journey. It has been a wonderful collaboration. The first book in the series, *The Psalms as Christian Worship* (2010), was followed by a second volume on *Psalms of Lament* (2014), and we now are concluding with *Psalms of Praise*.

Contemporary Collaborations

In 2016, Michael Parker and I wrote *The Challenge of the Aging Church*, to help the church face the explosive growth of the number of seniors, since medical science now can give us three more decades of life. My co-author Mike, a Lieutenant Colonel psychiatrist in the Army, had been in the Iraq War and dealt with post-traumatic stress among soldiers. As he and his comrades were preparing to return home, his rank entitled him to apply for a doctoral fellowship at Michigan State University. He felt called of God to switch specialties and become a geriatric psychiatrist, but his colleagues warned him the Medical General there in Baghdad would rebuff such a change of career. Fearfully he knocked at the general's office door, unaware that just half an hour before, the pastor to his aging mother in North Carolina had phoned about her dementia. "What can we do?" the pastor had asked, "about your mother leaving the hot plate red hot? She'll burn the house down!" Using definitely military language, the general shouted down the phone, "What the hell can I do, here in Baghdad?" Then Mike knocked timidly. "General," he said, "with the escalation of old people in our demographics, I feel called to change my career to becoming a geriatric psychiatrist." His timing was impeccable. The general answered, "'There's nothing nobler than doing this!"

In this context, Mike asked me to collaborate: to challenge churches to care for their seniors, not to treat them as retired "seniors" but as active "elders." I somewhat cynically defined the former group as "those who stir out their lives with coffee spoons at Starbucks in the morning, and their only monument lost golf balls, in the afternoon." We may need to send church groups of seniors on safari to some of the most primitive tribes of the Rift Valley in East Africa, the Hadza, to learn from their tribal elders what it is to be an "elder," passing on the wisdom of the past to the youth today. One benefactor actually did so (as recorded in M. Finkel, "The Hadza," in *National Geographic Magazine* in December 2009). We are also keenly aware that this gift of three more decades is increasing the population struggling with the effects of "dementias." (It is plural, for there are over a hundred types and causes of dementia.) As I lecture at dementia conferences, I now see how this deepens the Christian understanding of the incarnation, of Christ coming where we are, and entering into our mortality and its afflictions, as he also entered into our world of sin and death.

Celebration of Regent Alumni in Our Jubilee Year

In 2018, we celebrated the Jubilee of Regent College, since we started our first summer school in 1968. Partly in celebration, we recently published a book of essays written by some of our distinguished Regent College alumni and a few other scholars (forty-one in total), *Sources of the Christian Self: A Cultural History of Christian Identity*, celebrating all the wonderful things God has accomplished in their lives, in a blend of self-sacrifice and "minds on fire for God." Co-edited by my colleague Jens Zimmerman, a distinguished German philosopher, *Sources of the Christian Self* was a wonderful celebration for our Jubilee year. It describes how at pivotal points of history, great minds and souls have grappled with critical issues. That is the making of the prophetic voice, calling for repentance from the "old ways." The essays explain why "reform" is not enough; what is required is *metanoia*, a paradigm shift. Its mood is therefore apocalyptic. I am reminded of Malcolm Muggeridge's plenary address at the Lausanne Conference in 1974, "Living through an Apocalypse," referred to in an earlier chapter. In that address he observed, "It is sometimes difficult to resist the conclusion that Western Man has decided to abolish himself, creating his own boredom out of his own affluence, his own vulnerability out of his own strength, his own impotence out of his own eroto-mania ..." That was four decades ago, but his prophetic words are more relevant than ever. We now face the substitution of artificial intelligence for our own, and the rise of "Robotic Man" and the threat to planet Earth are not far behind. Only our amazing experiences of the grace of God keep me sleeping well at night!

Again by invitation, I was asked by an alumnus of the C. S. Lewis Institute, Theodore George, to collaborate with him on a book, *Freedom from Fear to Love*, uniting insights of neuroscience with other genres. As former head of Addiction in the National Institute of Health, Ted has located the basic physical source of fear in the upper brainstem, and as he explained, all our human emotions are motivated by fear. This book is in progress.

Chapter Seventeen

RECENT TRAVELS
IN THE FAR EAST

*I*n the human tapestry, old threads that we thought discarded can be picked up again and worked into new, unexpected designs. It has been that way with me, ever since the boredom I felt in our boardroom joint meetings of the university faculty of geography and anthropology. Yet cultural studies were always my *forte*, even in writing these memoirs, concerning the great cultural changes of the twentieth century. My visits to the Far East—China, Malaysia, Borneo, Papua New Guinea, Jakarta, Singapore, Honk Kong, Taiwan, and Japan—have been extensive since the 1980s, and Japanese Christians have taught me new perspectives on human emotions.

Liberating Japanese Women!

The first Japanese women students who attended Regent never returned home, for the new freedom they tasted in the West changed their lives. Five later students stayed in our home in turn, to be adopted by Rita as her "Japanese daughters." They did return home to Japan, but Rita's feisty spirit liberated their inner freedom more than any studies could have done. On our fiftieth wedding anniversary, which we celebrated in Tokyo on March 20, 2003, at a banquet in our honor, those ladies presented us both with fifty golden yellow roses, the imperial color.

Our daughter Claire has visited them frequently since then. Now in their own jubilee-plus years, Rita's "Japanese daughters" invited Claire to lead them in a three-day women's retreat in late April, 2017, and I too was invited. This was a new venture for me, though Claire has visited them yearly in her ministry. We addressed the issue of the adoration of Mary as an area in which evangelical circles can be said to have a defect. Evangelicals tend to confuse the Roman Catholic "Mariolotry" with the rightful adoration of Mary that all Christians should share. Protestants tend to ignore Mary in their hymns and prayers, again in reaction against the Roman Catholic custom of seeing her as "Mediatrix."

I suggest that this leads to downgrading womanhood in other chauvinistic ways. Indeed, in medieval areas (as in France) where customary law (not Roman law) prevailed, women were permitted to trade as merchants, as also in Sweden/Finland. In contrast, Roman-law countries such as Scotland and Switzerland were the last to give women the vote—as late as 1949 in some cantons of Switzerland, and only in 1984 in Liechtenstein. All this was quite new to the Japanese women, and I concluded by criticizing the definition of a Japanese woman as "she who walks three steps behind her man!" In the second session, I commended them for the wonderful aesthetic gift of Japanese women, of flower arrangements, gift-wrapping, their tea ceremonies, etc. Then I said, "Now Claire will tell you what I cannot describe." For Claire was just recovering from surgery for a brain tumor, so her forehead was gently covered by a discreet haircut and a bandeau, to hide a scar that marked her from ear to ear. "Jesus," she gently said, "did not choose to bear the body of the 'transfigured Lord' in Heaven; instead he chose to bear the scars of the crown of thorns he wore on the cross." By this time, the women were all softly weeping. The next session was a question-and-answer closure for the retreat, and their husbands and pastors were all clamoring to be present. "Hands up," I said, "for those of you who want the men to be present." Not a hand was raised. Then, clapping their hands, they shouted, "We are free!"

The next year, we returned to Tokyo, this time to address the cultural hindrances that make it difficult for Japanese people to receive the gospel. Quickly, I sensed my Western arrogance—for all cultures, East or West, are blinded from gladly receiving the gospel! Overnight, I changed my addresses, now to express my appreciation of what the West can learn from the benefits and richness of Japanese culture. This was published in a small book: *The Christian Life, East and West: Toward the Mutual Enrichment of Japanese and Western Christianity* (2017). Now I am returning to celebrate another book, this time in Japanese, on the distinct traits of Christian emotions that transcend our natural/cultural emotions globally: *The Uniqueness of "Christian Emotions*. This will be further elaborated (in English) in the context of other ancient cultures, in *Christian Emotions, as the Friends of Christ*.

A Mystical Experience
for a Change of Direction in Discipleship

At the end of 2017, I was flying across the Pacific, bone-weary, knowing that the next day, the first Sunday of Advent, December 9, I was to preach twice at the Methodist Cathedral in Singapore. We were due to land at midnight. I was praying, "Lord, whatever shall I preach tomorrow morning?" for I had prepared two plenary addresses but not the sermon. The music and words of Handel's "Messiah" began to surge through my sleepiness, "For unto us a child is born, unto us a Son is given" (Isa 9:6). The next morning I spoke on the text, saying that I had long ago questioned "systematic theology" as hyper-cognitive, and even "spiritual theology," which I had introduced to Evangelicals as more comprehensive, including our emotions as well as our minds. Now, I suggested we introduce a new realm, that of "child theology," as encompassing our humanity from childhood to death. As Guerric of Igny (a fellow Cistercian monk of Bernard of Clairvaux) had observed, "Christ did not humble Himself to become a Man; he came into the world as a little child!"

Three business ladies in their fifties were present, and they had brought a colleague, a secular Buddhist. She had scorned their repeated invitations to attend church services, but the day before I spoke, she had surprised them by asking, "Please, can you take me to church tomorrow?" Quietly, after the service, she said, "Now I am a Christian!"

I arranged to see her the next evening, asking with tears of joy, "Whatever happened to you?"

"It was very simple," she replied. "On Friday night, I was awakened from sleep, for the baby Jesus was placed on my bosom. Of course, I am now a Christian!"

Then I began to be challenged also. For do not the Gospels, especially Matthew and Mark, teach emphatically that becoming a disciple of Jesus is becoming as a child before him? Yet, over the history of Christianity, this voice has been lost. It needs to be heard again: "except you become as a little child, you cannot enter the kingdom of Heaven!" Now with the help of Kelly Lamb, I am editing a book of essays on "child theology," as a concept more comprehensive of the whole of our lives, from birth to death. This will explore biblically, theologically, historically, and from contemporary disciplines, how our personalities are shaped throughout life, resulting in new understandings of discipleship.

Chapter Eighteen

RITA, AS WIFE AND MOTHER

*M*argaret Isobel Davidson was born January 28, 1924, near East Kilbride, a suburb of Glasgow. She had three older sisters, Grace, Sheila, Nesta, and a younger brother, Don. She was named Isobel after an aunt who was wife to the last governor of Assam, before the Indian partition in 1947. But when she married she declared to all, she was now to be called "Rita," to the bewilderment of friends who had always known her as "Margaret." While her older sisters Grace and Nesta served in the war driving Red Cross ambulances, Rita finished her degree in education at Glasgow University, then went to Cambridge University to obtain her certificate to teach in private schools. She then went to Lausanne, as her mother had done, to spend two years there, first to teach a wealthy couple English, then to teach in a private finishing school for girls. It was a heavenly existence compared with post-war rationing in Britain, so, somewhat rebellious, she returned home for two stints of teaching in boys' private schools in Scotland. The rest of the story, of how we met and married, is told elsewhere.

Having rebelled as a teenager, with her younger brother, both close together, she wanted each of her three daughters to know they were each specified. At eleven years old, each girl went to a hotel, by train, as a special treat: Lydele to Weymoth on the south coast, where she was fascinated to help the concierge with his rows of bedroom keys; Claire to the Sussex coast for a music festival, giving her a sweet singing voice ever since; and Penny to an unremembered hotel, near which was a shoe factory, but which meant little to her, for she never needed the holiday— since, being the youngest, she always had extra time with Mum. She remembers coming home from school, having lunch alone together. She remembers Mum was always willing to drop everything (especially work) and to play, swim, and to have tea together. "I have always received her utter delight in my presence. Though she knew as well as I, my faults and shortcomings, they never seemed to matter."

Meanwhile, Christopher was left to his own devices at New College school, where as a choir boy he learnt to have a passion for choral music, which he still has. He designed much later in life an old cloister-chapel in his farmhouse, where recitals occur weekly with the St. John's Elora Choir in Ontario. But at school, he was bullied by a bad master. This toughened him to confront business leaders as a business management consultant, yet to be passionate about team management, which has always been his *forte*. But he never felt close to his mother as his sisters all did. Such are family memoirs; they all differ!

Chapter Nineteen

THE FAMILY
FACING RITA'S DEMENTIA

Dementia is one of the delayed processes of our mortality. With the advances of medical sciences giving many of us three more decades of life, dementia will increase exponentially and become explosive in our society. Rita's dementia lasted over ten years. As with so many families, it began with downsizing to a smaller home, and gradually to the spouse taking on more and more of the family duties. Again each child experienced it differently. Busy with his hard work and many travels, Christopher did not see much of his mother. Claire too, was travelling globally as a flight stewardess. But Mother was always sweet with her, conversing about what memories remained unimpaired. Towards the end, Rita would say on their walk, "I don't know who you are, but you know me." Penny too, recalled her Mother in her dementia, recognizing her but no longer remembering her name, and with excitement exclaiming in sheer delight, "It's YOU!" But Lydele bore the brunt of a frightened mother, scared at the loss of memory and of her identity, quickly angry and accusing her of many things.

Rita's dementia was dramatically traumatized on January 1, 2015, when our Grandson Jonathan Taylor announced his engagement to a church and school sweetheart, Amanda Kelsey. She was a medical student, and both were returning to Ottawa University after the Christmas holidays. On a snowy road, crossing a narrow icy bridge, an oncoming truck skidded into them, and killed them, pinning Amanda immediately. Jonathan, receiving the full impact on the driver's side, was badly injured, and helicoptered to Ottawa to save his life. Rita, hearing the news but unable to piece it all into one narrative, began to have panic attacks, and a week later was taken to the psychiatric ward at the General hospital. After a nightmarish six weeks, she was tranquilized, to be able to spend the last months of her life in a lovely private hospital, dying peacefully on October 8, 2015.

Chapter Twenty

WALKING
THROUGH THE VALLEY

Memoirs of Beloved Friends

*D*eath is a "no" word in our culture, but it should be as natural as *birth*. Indeed, I have accompanied two dear friends and my wife on "the walk through the valley of the shadow of death." As a Scot, I have loved the tune "Crimond" as mournfully beautiful (especially when conducted by Sir Hugh Roberton, with the Glasgow Orpheum choir singing Psalm 23). In previous ages of such high mortality rates, even of young children, this psalm developed its own immortality.

Sick at home in the summer of 1985, my good friend Elisabeth Bockmuehl told us that her husband Klaus had been diagnosed with the very painful esophageal cancer. He was operated on, and he persisted in his teaching and writing. But by October 1988, he became bedridden, and I promised to visit him every afternoon from then on. I missed only a three-week break during December, when I was away in Hong Kong. He died June 10, 1989.

Each day I brought him a promise from the Scriptures, until on one occasion, I felt I had nothing more to say. But I had been reading Julian of Norwich, so feeling rather foolish (before a scholarly theologian such as Klaus), I gave him a hazelnut, saying, "Klaus, Julian reminds us that as small as this nut is, 'God made it, for God cares for it, for God loves it.' Take it, then, and may it comfort you." After he died, it was found cracked with the pressures with which he sometimes held it, tucked under his pillow slip. His friends created "the fellowship of the hazelnut," one of whom, Gail Stevenson (1936–2018), became a close friend to his widow Elisabeth. She lovingly planted two hazel trees at the entrance to our home, to keep us steadily supplied with hazelnuts.

Having been a widow for ten years, that same friend Gail was told in early January 2018 that because of a leaking heart valve, she could not expect to live more than a few days or weeks. Since she was now living on Vancouver Island, I could not repeat the daily visits I had given Klaus, so I began to send her an email message every morning. Some of these may comfort you, dear reader, if you face the same challenge with a dying loved one.

March 4, 2018

Dear Gail,

One advantage we both share is that we have been widowed. We have witnessed the passing of a loved one. As you say in your beautiful poem "Goodbye," there is not a more final or heart-rending event than death. Yet as you add, "Nothing is so simple ... because it is of God." It is an exchange from pain to glory, from a time of life, to a life for eternity. ... I have been reflecting how contrasted our natural/cultural emotions are, with *Christian emotions*! The latter are described by William Blake:

Joy and woe are woven fine,
A clothing for the soul divine,
Under every grief and pine
Runs a joy with silken twine.

Christian emotions are the emotions of the Cross, of Suffering intermingled with Joy. For the end of the story is not dust, but Eternal Life, that it is all Love!

Love, Jim

March 16, 2018

Dear Gail,

Psalm 121 was one of Rita's favorites, as she looked out of our window to the mountains of the North Shore of Vancouver. "Mountains don't go away," she observed, "though the clouds may cover them, as if they never existed." But as the psalm indicates, our help comes from the Lord who made Heaven and Earth. He never sleeps, so He can always hear our cry. He provides the shade from the hot sun, and guides us with moonlight when it is dark. He preserves us from all evil, and whatever state we are in, He is there beside us.

The Romantic poet Samuel Taylor Coleridge, waiting for sunrise in the valley of Chamonix, saw Blanc rise as "a most awful form! Rising from the dark sea of pine forests, a terrifying sight," until:

… I look again,
It is thine own calm home, thy crystal shrine,
Thy habitation from eternity!

Love, Jim

Gail never knew Ernst and Erika van Eeghen, but on March 24, 2018, I quoted the comfort expressed by Ernst, which he had sent me, at the memorial for Erika:

Dear Gail,

I have been re-reading your mother's last letter to her children. It is so beautiful, as all being symbolic of a mother's love. Meditating on 2 Cor. 9:15, "Thanks be unto God, for His inexpressible Gift," Paul himself must have been meditating on the words of our Lord in the Upper Room: "Not as the world, give I unto you ... let not your hearts be troubled." Each of us is God's gift to the Other, so gladly we return the heirloom to the original Giver. My friend Ernst was pondering on this, after the death of his wife, and he sent this meditation to me:

> We give them back to Thee, dear Lord, who gavest them to us.
> Yet as You do not lose them in the giving, so we have not lost them by their return.
> Not as the world gives, givest Thou, O Lover of souls.
> What Thou gavest, Thou takest not away; for what is Thine, is ours always, if we are Thine.
> And Life is eternal, and Love is immortal, and death
> Is only the limit of our sight.
> Lift us up, strong Son of God, that we may see farther.
> Cleanse our eyes, that we may see more clearly. Amen

There followed this lovely prayer at Erika's memorial, from the same source:

> Draw us closer to Thyself that we may know ourselves
> nearer to our beloved who are with Thee. And while
> Thou dost prepare a place for us, prepare us for that
> Happy place, that where they are, and Thine art, we too
> May be:
> Through Jesus Christ, Amen
> The parting lies behind,
> The meeting lies before.

> Again, it would help, dear Gail, to know how conscious you are to receive these messages.
> Love, Jim

There was no further response from Gail. She died peacefully on the evening of April 3, 2018.

With my wife, Rita, the context was different. As I have mentioned in other books and lectures, I nursed her through dementia for more than ten years. As the mind shuts down, logical memory disappears, and only the sensory memory is left. On her last day, I simply held her hand for seventeen hours, knowing that she "knew" I was walking hand-in-hand with her, through the valley of the shadow of death with her, "all the way into the everlasting Kingdom." My son Chris and my eldest daughter Lydele were with me, bonded together ever deeper by our loss, yet so much closer to heaven. Again, my only surviving sister Ethel died this past November, in the process only to be bonded more closely with friends who dearly loved her. Now I have my eleventh great-grandchild, Arden James, which makes me so deeply aware of the unity of life and death. But far greater is the unity Christians have in the death and resurrection of Christ. I echo the words of an early twentieth-century Russian President 'D', formerly a Communist atheist: "It's dumb not being a Christian!"

People often ask me, "Do you miss Rita?"

"Not really," I reply.

Yes, I get choked up when I see a photo of her, or when some remark is made. For now, only a thin veil lies between us, for we are both in the presence of the Lord, she now eternally, and I, every time I awake in the morning, to say, "Thank you Lord, for the grace of another day to be in your presence!"

CONCLUSION

I conclude with a question: What has motivated and guided me this long life, nearing a centenary? Friends and opportunities have been like numerous road signals. But like celestial navigation by the polestar, several verses of the apostle Paul have enlightened and guided my life.

From my childhood days onwards, there has been the growing awareness that "my strength is made perfect in weakness" (2 Cor 12:9). "You then, my child, be strengthened by the grace which is in Christ Jesus" (2 Tim 2:1 ESV).

"O King Agrippa, I was not disobedient unto the heavenly vision" (Acts 26:19), as I was privileged to have, in late December 1961.

Rita and I celebrated our twenty-fifth wedding anniversary in Athens, on March 20, 1978. We stood on the hillside knoll, a spot, identified by a bronze plaque, where the apostle Paul had stood and was provoked in spirit that the city was full of idols. There, he testified with boldness in the shadow of the Acropolis, on Mars Hill, "Whom ... ye ignorantly worship, Him declare I unto you!" (Acts 17:23).

There, having read the passage inscribed on the plaque, we prayed together that we would never lack courage to be bold in our witness of Jesus Christ. It was like a renewal of our marriage vows, to encourage one another in our continual witness.

For many years now, as by the polestar, I have navigated by this pledge from Proverbs 4:18: "The path of the just is as the shining light, that shineth more and more unto the perfect day!" It gives serenity, like seeing an angel in the window of the soul. The older we grow, the more preoccupied we are with death, either trying to deny its existence or embracing it as entering into eternal life. For when Christ, dying on the cross, announced in a loud voice, "It is finished!" he meant that for God's eternal purpose to be fulfilled in us, we humans should become the *imago Dei*, his own image. That purpose was now accomplished by the death of God for the eternal life of humanity. That is why Christians glory in the cross of Christ, for death is a defeated foe, and our mortality has been exchanged for Christ's immortality. Hallelujah!

Since Rita's death on October 8, 2015, I constantly think of my pledge to her, as she entered dementia: "My dear, the loss of your memory gives me a gift from the Lord, to be your memory keeper! Now we are entering the golden years of our marriage!" Like the thief on the cross, I am comforted by his petition, "Jesus, remember me, when You come into your Kingdom" (Luke 23:42 ESV)

God needs no memoirs, no reminders. Only we do.

CPSIA information can be obtained
at www.ICGtesting.com
Printed in the USA
LVHW110319220120
644343LV00001B/1